09444

Information Centre & Library

D0830684

THE AMBIGUITIES OF EXPERIENCE

The Messenger Lectures

A book from

The Center for the Study of
Economy & Society
Cornell University

THE AMBIGUITIES OF EXPERIENCE

James G. March

Cornell University Press
Ithaca and London

First published 2010 by Cornell University Press

Printed in the United States of America

Library of Congress Cataloging-in-Publication Data

March, James G.
The ambiguities of experience / James G. March.
p. cm.
Includes bibliographical references and index.
ISBN 978-0-8014-4877-5 (cloth : alk. paper)
1. Organizational learning. 2. Experience—Social aspects.
3. Intelligence—Social aspects. I. Title.
HD58.82.M3668 2010
302.3′5—dc22 2009036384

Cornell University Press strives to use environmentally responsible suppliers and materials to the fullest extent possible in the publishing of its books. Such materials include vegetable-based, low-VOC inks and acid-free papers that are recycled, totally chlorine-free, or partly composed of nonwood fibers. For further information, visit our website at www.cornellpress.cornell.edu.

Cloth printing 10 9 8 7 6 5 4 3 2 1

CONTENTS

PREFACE

The chapters in this book are based on three Messenger Lectures given at Cornell University in October 2008. I am grateful to the university and particularly to my hosts, Victor Nee and Danielle Adams, who made the visit a pleasure for me. Parts of the material are based on talks I have given at Harvard University, the Massachusetts Institute of Technology, and the University of California, Irvine. For their able assistance in preparing the manuscript for publication, I owe thanks to three Cornell University Press editors: Roger Haydon, Priscilla Hurdle, and Ange Romeo-Hall, as well as to Jamie Fuller. The index was prepared by Daniel Newark.

The book focuses on a few small aspects of a simple question: What is, or should be, the role of experience in creating intelligence, particularly in organizations? The chapters presented here are intended to provide fragments of a partial answer to that question. The fragments represent a sampler of possible ideas rather than a comprehensive encyclopedia of them. They provide incomplete ruminations on the ideas rather than thorough expositions of them. The small number of words in the book may be somewhat balanced by the large number of references (a testimony to authorial inadequacy), including an excessive number of self-references (a testimony to authorial self-indulgence).

Although they might with justice claim that I have extracted lessons from their teachings that are not what they intended, seven talented colleagues and friends have contributed substantially to the ideas here and must share some of the blame: Mie Augier, who bridges the chasms among Schütz, Kundera, Plath, Nietzsche, and Dosi with a combination of enthusiasm and skepticism that I admire; Barbara Czarniawska, who has tried patiently for many years to teach me about stories, narratives, and organization theory; Jerker Denrell, who has made my life better through conversations about endogenous sampling, learning, and the wonders of stochastic processes; Daniel Levinthal, with whom I have shared many years of conversation and collaboration on problems of organizational learning; Johan P. Olsen, whose wisdom, careful scholarship, and friendship inform everything I do, and particularly the topics covered here; William H. Starbuck, whose contributions to understanding the problems and possibilities of learning in organizations span almost as many years as mine; and Sidney Winter, whose reluctance to write his thoughts is matched only by their fruitfulness when he gets around to it. I will not try to list the many others to whom I owe debts. I once did that, and it took up several pages of text.

I have benefited from generous financial support by the Spencer Foundation, the Reed Foundation, the Stanford Graduate School of Business, the Stanford University School of Education, and the Copenhagen School of Business. I appreciate both their support and the spirit of free inquiry in which it has been provided.

Finally, I owe a large debt to the infinite tolerance of my wife, Jayne. With a grace that suggests some rare variety of benevolence, she has borne my presence for over sixty years. It is an achievement as inexplicable as it is appreciated.

JAMES G. MARCH

Stanford University, December 2009

THE AMBIGUITIES OF EXPERIENCE

1
THE PURSUIT OF INTELLIGENCE

Organizations pursue intelligence. It is not a trivial goal. Its realization is imperfect, and the pursuit is endless. Every day there are failures to temper any successes. Nevertheless, the pursuit is often exhilarating. It exalts the subtle textures of life and elevates coping with ordinary tasks to the artistry of history. The present book considers one aspect of the pursuit of intelligence—the effort to extract lessons from the unfolding episodes of life. Organizations and the individuals in them try to improve by contemplating and reacting to their experiences.

Folk wisdom both trumpets the significance of experience and warns of its inadequacies. On the one hand, experience is described as the best teacher. On the other hand, experience is described as the teacher of fools, of those unable or unwilling to learn from accumulated knowledge or the teaching of experts. The disagreement between the folk aphorisms reflects profound questions about the human pursuit of intelligence through learning from experience that have long confronted philosophers and social scientists.

Despite extensive enthusiasm for it, the prima facie evidence for organizational improvement through extracting lessons from experience is mixed. Contemporary organizations certainly engage in practices, follow procedures, and exhibit forms that are notably different from organizations of a century ago. By most measures of productivity, contemporary organizations are more efficient than their predecessors. At the same time, experience is often ambiguous and the inferences to be drawn from it are unclear; and the contribution of experiential learning to long-term improvements in organizations is difficult to establish. The ambiguity of history makes the matching of beliefs and actions to experience both complicated and prone to misdirection (March and Olsen 1975; 1995, chap. 6).

There are well-documented cases of the apparent failure of organizations to adapt to their environments. Failures of business firms to copy successful practices from other firms are a familiar refrain of organizations research. Wars are filled with instances of what appears, with the clear vision of after-the-fact perspicacity, to be organizational blindness on the part of armies. The hugely successful American steel and automobile industries of the first half of the twentieth century withered in the last half. The American public school system changed from being the pride of the country and the envy of other countries to being an embarrassment. The American political system found it difficult to adapt to declines in American prosperity and power as the twenty-first century began.

While acknowledging the power of learning from experience and the extensive use of experience as a basis for adaptation and for constructing stories and models of history, the chapters in this book examine particularly the problems with such learning. The essays argue that although individuals and organizations are eager to derive intelligence from experience, the inferences stemming from that eagerness are often misguided. The problems lie partly in correctable errors of human inference forming, but they lie even more in properties of experience that confound learning from it (March 2008, chap. 5). As a result, the book is somewhat more conservative about the possibilities for experiential learning than is characteristic of some writings about it (Kolb 1984; Sternberg and Wagner 1986; Kayes 2002). It identifies some endemic ambiguities and mistakes of experience.

PROLEGOMENON

The ideas pursued in this book reflect three rather different traditions of scholarship. The first is the tradition of scholarship on organizations. That tradition draws particularly from economics, psychology, management science, sociology, political science, public administration, and artificial intelligence. For the most part, scholars within the tradition are Cartesian, scientific, and analytical. They emphasize the formal analysis of data and testing of hypotheses, exercising models, and proving theorems. They are prone to deductive cleverness in the form of relatively limited but provocative ideas, as reflected in enthusiasms for such things as game theory, cognitive dissonance, structural equivalence, absorptive capacity, and garbage-can theories. They practice a style of analysis that focuses on relatively simple relations among discrete variables. They speak, for the most part, from the perspective of the social and behavioral science establishments. And they presume a history that moves haltingly toward greater knowledge and intellectual progress.

The second tradition is that of scholarship on storytelling, narrative, and myth. These humanistic traditions of scholarship draw particularly from literature, criticism, history, anthropology, linguistics, legal studies, and religion. They emphasize language, metaphor, and the elaboration of meaning. Like Dario Fo, who emulates the jesters of the Middle Ages, attacking authority and glorifying the dignity of the downtrodden, many of them place themselves in opposition to the establishment. They are prone to expansive speculation in the form of sweeping generalizations in the manner of Freud, Marx, or Foucault but also revel in close investigation of the human estate in its fine detail. They practice a style of scholarship that exploits the nuances of language to evoke meanings. And they generally eschew notions of intellectual progress in favor of ideas of intellectual and historical embeddedness, social construction, and cultural consciousness.

The third tradition is that of scholarship on adaptive processes. Although the work is intertwined with empirical studies of change, it is heavily theoretical. It emphasizes properties of the mechanisms of adaptation in organisms, species, technologies, organizations, industries, and societies. The traditions of research on adaptation draw heavily from evolutionary biology and psychological ideas about human learning. They attempt to further understanding by identifying adaptive processes and exploring their consequences in complex ecologies of multiple adapting agents. They pay particular attention to the capabilities of adaptive processes to realize outcomes that are, in some meaningful sense, improvements—even optimal. They generally presume a historical process that is heavily history-dependent with multiple unstable equilibria, but an intellectual process that allows some elements of nonrandom forward movement.

The chapters in this book draw copiously and inadequately from all three traditions, but they focus on a relatively narrow topic: When and how do organizations learn intelligently from their experience? What are the possibilities and problems? The chapters address such issues, but they hardly resolve them. They have all the limitations and perversities of brevity.

Among other limitations, strictly organizational factors in organizational learning from experience are subordinated in these chapters to the ambiguous features of experience, the structural features of adaptive processes, and the intellective features of human adaptation. Organizational factors are discussed from time to time, but there is no attempt to be exhaustive with respect to them. The subordination is one of convenience, not a symptom of unimportance. Organizations shape the way experience unfolds and the way in which it is observed and comprehended. They define the networks through which information flows and reinforce or reduce the cleavages of conflict. They create and maintain the goals and expectations that calibrate aspirations. They are systems of rules, routines, capabilities, and identities that both resist and record the lessons of experience. Such factors can be ignored only as a temporary expediency, and even so at some risk.

In addition, three critical properties of organizational adaptation that are vital to a thorough understanding are not considered significantly here. First, organizations are coalitions of conflicting interests (March 1988, chap. 5; Hoffman 1999; Rao, Morrill, and Zald 2000). Conflicts of interest make theories of conflict-free adaptation notoriously incomplete, complicating particularly the association of success or failure with outcomes and the pooling of information (Cyert and March 1963; Augier and March 2001). Conflicts of interest are conspicuous factors in all organizations and influence not only the pursuit of intelligence but also its definition (Greenwood, Suddaby, and Hinings 2002; Olsen 2009).

Second, organizational adaptation involves the simultaneous, interacting adaptation of several nested levels (March 1994, chaps. 2, 6; Friedland and Alford 1991). Populations of organizations evolve at the same time as the individual organizations within the populations, and organizations evolve at the same time as individuals within the organizations. These nested systems of adaptation affect each other, with adaptation at one level sometimes serving as a substitute for adaptation at another and sometimes interfering with it.

Third, the environment of organizations consists, in part, in other adapting organizations; and the elements of coevolution produced by their simultaneous adjustments are an essential feature of the adaptive story (Hannan and Freeman 1989; Kauffman and Johnsen 1992; Levinthal and Myatt 1994). The treatment of the environment as exogenous, as is common in the literature on organizational learning and, to a substantial extent, in these chapters, is a significant simplification.

TWO COMPONENTS OF INTELLIGENCE

Intelligence normally entails two interrelated but somewhat different components. The first involves effective adaptation to an environment. In order to adapt effectively, organizations require resources, capabilities at using them, knowledge about the worlds in which they exist, good fortune, and good decisions. They typically face competition for resources and uncertainties about the future. Many, but possibly not all, of the factors determining their fates are outside their control. Populations of organizations and individual organizations survive, in part, presumably because they possess adaptive intelligence; but survival is by no means assured. Although a few organizations, most notably the Roman Catholic Church and older European universities, have survived for many years, the vast majority of organizations endure for only a relatively short time. By that criterion, at least, organizational adaptive intelligence is not guaranteed. It is not even typical.

The second component of intelligence involves the elegance of interpretations of the experiences of life. Such interpretations encompass both theories of history and philosophies of meaning, but they go beyond such things to comprehend the grubby details of daily existence. The desire of human beings to make sense of their experiences permeates much of scholarship. It also permeates much of life. Interpretations of experience are ornaments of casual conversations and of theories of psychological, economic, political, cultural, and social systems. Stylishness of interpretation is a certification of human status and a basis for the social ranking of individuals and institutions. Interpretations decorate human existence. They make a claim to significance that is independent of their contribution to effective action. Raymond Fischesser, a former director of L'École des mines de Paris, defined intelligence as "la préoccupation efficace de l'essentiel" (Riveline 2008, 7). Such intelligence glories in the contemplation, comprehension, and appreciation of life, not just the control of it.

EXPERIENTIAL LEARNING

The tools for achieving intelligence reflect the knowledge technologies of the time and place. At some not-too-distant times and places, intelligence seeking involved extensive use of magic potions, enchantments, and incantations, as well as the anticipations and ambiguities of oracles and other keepers of extrahuman capabilities. No self-respecting manager of early Chinese, Egyptian, Greek, or Roman enterprise would have willingly confronted the uncertainties of life without a suitable pipeline to the gods who manipulated the universe within which their organizations operated.

Though various forms of godlike revelation continue to secure adherents (Eisenstadt 2006), efforts to access the mysteries of the gods have been largely replaced in modern life by efforts to uncover more mundane secrets of knowledge. In that respect, few ideas are as sacrosanct in contemporary sensibilities as the notion that human beings achieve mastery over their lives through learning from experience. Individuals and organizations try to improve their lots by observing and reacting to their experiences, partly by elementary efforts to reproduce actions associated with success, partly by more elaborate efforts to fit the events of their histories into acceptable causal frames. Experience is venerated; experience is sought; experience is interpreted.

Learning from experience is, of course, by no means the only mechanism of human learning. Indeed, most of what is known by individuals and organizations is not discovered in lessons extracted from the ordinary course of life and work. It is generated by systematic observation and analysis by experts and transmitted by authorities (e.g., in books, through web browsers, by teachers), and accepted (or rejected) without direct experiential confirmation. It reflects, in a general way, academic knowledge rather than experiential knowledge (March 2004).

Nevertheless, in the contemporary literature on organizations, experiential learning continues to be seen as one of the more important sources of adaptation in human action, a mechanism for improving the fit of actions by individuals or organizations to the environments they face (Argyris and Schön 1978; Levitt and March 1988; Huber 1991; Payne, Bettman, and Johnson 1993; Cohen and Sproull 1996; Argote 1999; Nooteboom 2000; Starbuck and Hedberg 2001; Greve 2003). Admirable organizations are described as "learning organizations"; advisers on ways to augment and refine learning abound (Argyris and Schön 1978; Senge 1990); and recent proposals for improving organizations have often emphasized learning from experience (Senge 1990; Olsen and Peters 1996; Dierkes et al. 2001; Zollo and Winter 2002).

Learning from experience is seen as relevant to theories of rational action (Arrow 1972; Coleman 1990; Milgrom and Roberts 1992) as found in game theory (von Neumann and Morgenstern 1944; Luce and Raiffa 1957; Kreps 1990b) and in decision theory (Raiffa 1968; Machina 1987; Anand 1993; Augier and March 2002). It is also seen as relevant to theories of rule-based action (March and Olsen 1989, chap. 2; March 1994, chap. 2) as found in ideas of individual identity, institutions, and social roles. In rational theories, the presumed fundamental basis of intelligent action is a logic of consequences (March and Olsen 1989, chap. 1; March 1994, chap. 1); in rule following, action follows from systems of rules, identities, and roles (Scott and Meyer 1983; Ashforth and Mael 1989; North 1990; Becker 2004; Brandstätter, Gigerenzer, and Hertwig 2006); and the presumed fundamental basis is a logic of appropriateness (Günther 1993; March and Olsen 2006b). Within both perspectives, experiential knowledge is seen as a necessary component of human claims to intelligence. In rational action, organizations are seen as looking forward by looking backward (Gavetti and Levinthal 2000; Zollo and Winter 2002; Gibbons and Roberts 2008). In rule-based action, organizational rules are seen as evolving through experience (Alchian 1950; Nelson and Winter 1982; March, Schulz, and Zhou 2000; Akerlof and Kranton 2005; March and Olsen 2006a).

Thus, considerable effort has been devoted to augmenting the effectiveness of intelligence in organizations by drawing on the evidence of history. Sophisticated instruments of estimation, modeling, and strategic planning have been created and implemented to facilitate marketing, financial, production, and human resource decision making in business firms and to facilitate the efficient and effective delivery of social services in governmental agencies. Elaborate systems of accounts have been developed to facilitate control over organizations by various stakeholders. Very large industries of consultants have arisen to diffuse practices and theories deemed useful. Schools of management have become conspicuous components of modern universities, providing education to large numbers of would-be future managers of both public and private organizations. Management education provides a menu of "good practices," as well as a kit of theories of markets, politics, operations, and firms.

In order to improve their fit to their environments, organizations frequently undertake changes in organizational practices, procedures, and forms. To be sure, the alternative possibility that the fit of an organization to its environment can be improved more easily by changing the environment than by changing the organization is reflected in strategies common among powerful players. From this perspective, adaptation is for the weak; the strong impose themselves and let others adapt to them. The great empires of history (Rome, China, Ottoman, Spain, Great Britain, the Soviet Union, the United States) have all thrived in part by forcing their environments to adapt to them, rather than wasting energy in trying to adapt to their environments. The same thing is true of the great industrial empires (US Steel, General Motors, Royal Dutch Shell, Unilever, Sony, IBM, Microsoft). It is true also of the human species. The long run disadvantage of improving fit by changing the environment is—as all of the examples illustrate—a decay of the ability to adapt to the environment if necessary, a decay that accelerates decline if a dominant position is lost.

The search for aids to experiential learning in organizations has been paralleled by a substantial empirical and theoretical effort in organization studies to develop theoretical ideas about the realities of organizational adaptation. That effort has been directed toward understanding the ways in which populations of organizations and individual organizations change (not necessarily intentionally) over time in response to adaptive pressures (Aldrich 1979; Cohen and Sproull 1996; Nooteboom 2000; Dierkes et al. 2001; Greve 2003; Aldrich and Ruef 2006; Dosi and Marengo 2007). Studies of the birth and death processes of organizational life and the resulting features of organizational demography have provided important contributions to these efforts (Hannan and Freeman 1989; Carroll and Hannan 2000).

This history of scholarship forms a background for the explorations in the present chapters. The chapters consider the complications involved in learning from experience. Some of these complications reflect well-known human information-processing habits—for example, biases toward conserving belief, simple causalities, historical certainty, and attributions of significance to human intentions. Those characteristics of human behavior are important, but the focus here is primarily on a separate set of the complications that reflect interactions between experience and the processes of learning. As the following chapters will argue, these problems lie primarily not in the learners but in the nature of experience.

2
LEARNING THROUGH REPLICATING SUCCESS

Extracting lessons from natural experience presumes a learning cycle that begins with observing associations between actions and outcomes, the rudiments of finding order in history. Learning takes place when the observation of associations produces changes in actions or rules for actions. Learning serves intelligence when those changes improve the actions or the rules. Changes from learning occur often and relatively easily, but their contribution to intelligence is more problematic. Experiential learning makes many mistakes.

TWO MODES OF INTELLIGENT ADAPTATION

It is useful to distinguish two different modes of achieving intelligence through experience. The two modes reflect different kinds of processes and encounter different kinds of complications, so the distinction may be useful as long as it is recognized that actual occasions of learning involve mixtures of the two (Zollo and Winter 2002; Winter, Cattani, and Dorsch 2007; Starbuck, Barnett, and Baumard 2008; Winter 2009). The first mode—which might be called "low-intellect" learning—is one in which actions associated with success are replicated with little or no effort at causal understanding. The second mode—which might be called "high-intellect" learning—is one in which explicit efforts are made to understand the causal structure of the events of experience and to derive action implications from that understanding. The distinction is closely related to that made by Starbuck, Barnett, and Baumard (2008) between noncognitive and cognitive learning and by Gul and Pesendorfer (2008) and Camerer (2008) between mindless and mindful economics, though the different terms contain somewhat different nuances. Low intellect and high intellect are not differentiated by merit. Each has its place; each has its limitations.

Low-intellect mechanisms of learning from experience are built on the replication of success and are common among both humans and other animal species. They often generate rules or heuristics of behavior that are surprisingly effective (Hutchinson and Gigerenzer 2005). High-intellect mechanisms, on the other hand, appear to be less prominent in the learning of other animals than they are among human beings. The entire academic apparatus for developing, recording, and dispensing knowledge derived from theories about the underlying causes of outcomes of experienced history is a distinctively human construction. That apparatus depends on the power of written language and instruments of symbolic manipulation that not only are uniquely human but have existed among humans only for the past few thousand years.

THE REPLICATION OF SUCCESS

The basic idea of replication of success is inherent in a familiar set of ideas in studies of organizations. Organizations are often seen as comparing performance with an aspiration for performance and searching for changes primarily when performance falls below aspiration (Cyert and March 1963; Greve 2003; Baum and Dahlin 2007). Thus, actions associated with success are more likely to be reproduced than are actions associated with failure.

In its barest form, the replication of success is elegant in its simplicity:

(1) Act by choosing an alternative from among those available.
(2) Record a result and evaluate it in terms of its success.
(3) Replicate the choice of alternatives associated with successes more often than the choice of alternatives associated with failure.

Practices, forms, and rules that are associated with good outcomes survive longer and reproduce more than practices, forms, and rules that are associated with poor outcomes.

It should be observed that describing the replication of success as low-intellect (or "noncognitive") is potentially misleading. Such a description ignores cognitive complications involved in the adaptive process. For example, in a classic binary learning task, a learner chooses repeatedly between two mutually exclusive and exhaustive alternatives. When consistently rewarded on one of the alternatives, the learner normally learns to choose it. However, even as elementary a situation as a T-maze leaves the cognitive definition of the alternatives unspecified. For example, are the two alternatives "go left" or "go right"? Or are they "go to the same place as last time" or "go to the other place"? The classic Bush-Mosteller-Estes model of learning in two-choice situations (Bush and Mosteller, 1955) predicts quite different learning patterns depending on the definition of the alternatives if the reward schedule alternates rewards on the two alternatives (Lave and March, 1975).

The intellect (cognitive) component becomes even more obvious when discussions of replication turn to issues concerning the generalization of learning to situations that are not identical to those in which previous experience has occurred but might be imagined to be, in some sense, similar (Winter 2009). "Similarity" can be provided a somewhat objective meaning in experimental settings; but in the real world it becomes a mental construct of considerable indeterminacy. Issues such as these are, for the most part, ignored in the discussion below.

The paradigmatic situation for the replication of success is one in which a choice is made repeatedly among a number of alternatives. The alternatives might be actions, strategies, products, technologies, locations, partners, or any number of other mutually exclusive and exhaustive items. In each time period, a particular alternative is chosen and an outcome is experienced. Subsequent choices favor alternatives associated with better past outcomes over alternatives associated with poorer outcomes. The capability generated by the replication of success is contextual. It may generalize to new situations that are, in some sense, similar to the original situation; but there is little reason to expect it necessarily to do so. And the capability reflects no significant element of causal understanding.

A process that simply replicates success is attractive for many reasons. It captures truth without the necessity of articulating it. It is a democratic instrument, being as accessible to the weak as to the powerful, as accessible to the uneducated as to the educated. It is a practical instrument, dealing more with the pragmatic necessities of ordinary life than with the abstract imaginations of ideas and theories. It is a tailored instrument, reflecting considerations in a specific concrete situation by virtue of having been developed in the same context. It is a compelling instrument, mobilizing a sense of personal relevance by its link to success and failure in direct experience.

Three Mechanisms

The replication of success may occur in a number of different ways. In particular, we consider three classic mechanisms. The three mechanisms differ in important ways, but they also share common structural features that are significant.

The first mechanism is *trial-and-error learning.* Learning replicates success by modifying rules so as to repeat successful actions more readily than unsuccessful actions. The paradigmatic experiential trial-and-error learning situation involves a set of alternatives with associated outcome distributions and a learning rule that modifies actions as a result of realized outcomes. There are two enormous literatures dealing with trial-and-error learning. The first is the literature on so-called bandit problems in operations research (Gittins 1989). A bandit problem is one involving sequential choices among a collection of alternatives with unknown payoff distributions. Information about a specific alternative can be obtained only by choosing it. The usual objective of the research on bandit problems is to find an optimal strategy for engaging such situations, or at least a strategy that is better than other known ones. The key strategic question is whether to select the apparently best alternative (on the basis of experience to date) or to sample alternatives further in order to gather more information. In general, the research on bandit problems indicates that optimal strategies depend on the time horizon chosen. The longer the time horizon, the more advantageous is the expanded sampling of unknown or apparently inferior alternatives.

The second enormous literature on trial-and-error learning deals with reinforcement learning in a T-maze (Mowrer and Klein 2001; Lovie 2005). The objective of the research is to understand animal and human learning in simple choice situations under various conditions of reward, and to model that learning. In general, the research indicates that learners characteristically improve performance as experience increases but that there are numerous situations in which choices that are made do not conform to what appears to be optimal behavior. For example, consider a situation in which there are two alternatives with probabilities of reward unknown to the learner but one with a probability p_1 of reward and the other with a probability $p_2 < p_1$ of reward. Many experiments of this sort have been run, leading to numerous attempts to confirm or disconfirm expected utility hypotheses about human behavior or specify the conditions under which they hold. For example, if the outcome for each alternative on each trial is revealed regardless of which alternative is chosen, an expected utility-maximizing learner would adopt a strategy of always choosing the more frequently rewarded alternative. Such a result is not always observed.

The second mechanism for replicating success is *imitation*. Imitation replicates success by having actions associated with success when executed by one actor imitated by another actor. Replication through imitation probably represents the majority of what is normally called "innovation" in the organizations literature (Mansfield 1961; Mahajan and Wind 1986). The ways in which known attributes and processes spread within a population of organizations have been studied extensively in research on innovation and change in organizations (Reinganum 1989; Haunschild and Miner 1997). The empirical study of imitation is complicated by the difficulty of distinguishing the aggregate results of a diffusion process from the often similar aggregate results of the independent adoption of a practice, product, or form in a heterogeneous population (Gray 1973; Volden, Ting, and Carpenter 2008). There seems little doubt, however, that imitation is often involved in the replication of success (Holden 1986; Conell and Cohn 1995).

The idea that things spread among organizations is well known in discussions of fashion and fads (Abrahamson 1991; Newell, Swan, and Kautz 2001; Kieser 2002), contagion (Burt 1987; Galaskiewiecz and Burt 1991; Strang and Soule 1998), and institutionalization (Zucker 1987; Bergevärn, Mellemvik, and Olson 1998; Scott 2003; Greenwood and Suddaby 2006). Studies of imitation emphasize the ways in which the successful actions of one actor are replicated in the actions of another (Miller and Dollard 1941; Nehaniv and Dautenhahn 2007) and the ways in which networks of associations affect the spread of ideas, beliefs, routines, or actions through a population (Podolny, Stuart, and Hannan 1996; Powell, Koput, and Smith-Doerr, 1996; Uzzi 1996).

Studies of replication through imitation build on standard epidemiological representations that assume the following (Bartholomew 1982):

(1) a set of alternatives with associated outcome distributions;

(2) a direct contact matrix that indicates the direct contacts for each actor; and

(3) a contagion rule that defines the likelihood of actor i imitating actor j at time t.

The prototypic models examine the replication of the behavior of the successful who are connected (Granovetter and Soong 1983; Strang and Soule 1998). The results depend on properties of the "donor" and the "recipient," properties of the "disease," and properties of the structure of linkage. In general, diffusion processes often exhibit threshold effects (Schelling 1971; Gladwell 2000), and they more reliably yield convergence (but see Greenwood and Suddaby 2006; Purdy and Gray 2009) than they do optimality (Strang and Macy, 2001). The effectiveness of imitation in finding optimal solutions depends on the structure of connections among learners; but it is not, in general, true that effectiveness increases monotonically with the density of connections.

Simple epidemiological conceptions embrace two assumptions that are particularly problematic when applied to replication among organizations. The first problematic assumption is that an object of diffusion is invariant as it diffuses. Studies of the spread of things among organizations indicate that the object of diffusion often is transformed as it is transferred from one organization to another (Czarniawska and Sevón 1996; Scott 2003). In fact, the ability to copy exactly is sometimes described as an essential feature of effective replication in organizations (Winter 2009). The second problematic assumption is that the links among adopters are unchanged by the process. In populations of organizations, the connections themselves are likely to be affected by the history of the diffusion process.

In particular, an instance of imitation is likely to strengthen the linkage through which the imitation occurs (March 1999a).

The third mechanism for replication of success is *selection.* Selection replicates success by reproducing attributes (e.g., rules, routines, forms) associated with success and eliminating attributes associated with failure. Theories of replication through selection assume a set of fixed attributes, a selection rule that determines survival among the attributes, and replication rules that determine the reproduction of attributes. In the organizational versions of replication through selection, the elimination of attributes depends on relative performance within a group of competitors, and successful attributes are replicated more often than unsuccessful ones (Alchian 1950; Winter 1964; Baum and Singh 1994).

These ideas, of course, draw upon other enormous literatures in evolutionary biology and evolutionary economics (Mayr 1963, 1982; Selten 1991; Gould 2002; Nelson and Winter 2002; Witt 2003). They posit various forms of variation in attributes and various processes of selection among them. The results depend on the specific forms taken by variation and selection and the nature of competition. The processes are generally slow relative to the changes in the environment to which they respond; and they often have multiple equilibria, not all of them equally attractive.

Two Sets of Questions

The literature on processes of adaptation that replicate success addresses two related, but different, sets of questions.

The first set includes: What *do* individuals or organizations do in this situation? How do they act? How do their actions change over time as a result of experience? To what extent, in what way, and at what rate do they respond to knowledge of experienced results? To what extent do they learn to pursue the best alternative?

The second set of questions includes: What *should* an intelligent person or organization do in this situation? How long should several alternatives be sampled in order to obtain information about them? When should a choice be made and on what basis?

With respect to the second set of questions, mechanisms for the replication of success share a fundamental problem that is also conspicuous in calculative rationality—indeed, in all adaptive processes: How do they recognize and achieve an optimal balance between exploitation and exploration? (See Kuhn 1962, 1977; Holland 1975; March 1999c, chap. 7; Chen and Katila 2008; Fang and Levinthal 2009.) Exploitation refers to the utilization and refinement of what is known. It is reflected in efforts toward efficiency, standardization, accountability, and control. Exploration is the pursuit of what is not known. It is reflected in efforts to generate and experiment with deviant procedures and new possibilities. In processes involving the replication of success, the problem is typically a problem of allocating resources between efforts to learn more about the world (exploration) and efforts to take advantage of what is already known (exploitation). A frequent question about the replication of success is whether, as it responds to immediate feedback, it allocates too few resources to exploration (Starbuck, Greve, and Hedberg 1978; Miller 1994).

There are some obvious criteria that can be applied to evaluate the effect of replicating success on any particular set of rules for action:

Improvement: Does average performance improve with experience?

Stability: Does the likelihood that a choice at time t repeats the choice at t−1 increase with experience?

Reputation error: Is the past realized performance (reputation) of the chosen alternative greater or less than its expected value? How does the error change with time?

Optimality: Is the best alternative discovered and adopted? How long does it take? Or alternatively, how close is the chosen alternative to the optimum in expected performance over time?

COMPLICATIONS IN SUCCESS REPLICATION

Trial-and-error learning, imitation, and selection have different properties as adaptive mechanisms, but they have a set of basic structural elements in common. These shared elements and the complications they create are the primary foci of the present discussion. For the most part, the phenomena considered here stem from properties of the learning environment and the adaptive mechanisms, not from any distinctive features of the cognitive apparatus that may be brought to bear on them. Thus they are different from, and substantially independent of, well-known cognitive limitations of individuals. These "structural" complications can be understood, but an understanding of the complications by an adaptive agent does not eliminate the difficulties.

First, history is complex. Even though the world may be orderly in the sense of following immutable laws, it is filled with complex causal relations. Forming correct inferences about history in the face of such complexity requires a complicated experimental design, a multivariate model, and a large sample. Unfortunately, the conditions underlying the replication of success in real experience include simple implicit experimental designs, simple implicit correlational models, and small samples. As a result, the replication of success is subject to extensive elements of misspecification and superstition.

Second, history is subject to stochastic uncertainty. The orderliness of the world is obscured by probabilistic variations. Identifying the best alternative through experience involves untangling the joint consequences of signal, noise, and sample size. *Signal:* The greater the true differences among alternatives, the greater the chance of identifying the true optimum by observing a sample. *Noise:* The smaller the stochastic variation in the observed outcomes, the greater the chance of identifying the true optimum by observing a sample. *Sample size:* The larger the sample, the greater the chance of identifying the true optimum by observing a sample.

Since experience in organizations often suffers from weak signals, substantial noise, and small samples, it is quite likely that realized history will deviate considerably from the underlying reality. Adaptation responds, not to the distribution of potential histories but to the specific history realized in a small sample. The results may lead to a more favorable experience with an alternative than is warranted, thus leading to a mistaken replication. Alternatively, the results may lead to a less favorable experience than is warranted, thus leading to a mistaken avoidance of replication.

As is well known to students of stochastic processes, stochastic variation produces some quite striking, counterintuitive surprises (Feller 1968). Many of these surprises are variations on so-called first-passage theorems or competitive maximum theorems. An example of the former is the case of coin flips: If a single fair coin is flipped a large number of times, what is the distribution of length of runs in which more than half of the results are heads? The usual intuition is that a fair coin should lead to relatively short runs of dominance by either heads or tails; the actual result is that the runs are, on average, rather long.

An example of competitive maximum theorems is provided by comparing two identical competitors, each of whom realizes each period a draw from a normal distribution with mean=0 and variance=1. Suppose we consider the average realized performance of the two competitors over time. As experience accumulates, the likelihood increases that the competitor with the greater average realized return at time t will also have the greater average realized return at t+1. That likelihood becomes quite high as t increases. The rankings of two competitors, in terms of average performance to date, persist for an extended time even though the two are identical in capabilities and even though the difference in average performance declines.

Third, the outcome possibilities for the various alternatives are affected by the sequence of choices made and the outcomes realized. Replication of success naturally affects the alternative chosen and thus the distribution of possibilities from which an outcome is drawn. Less obviously, it also often affects the distribution of possibilities for a given alternative. In standard terminology, the individual outcome distributions are endogenous to the choice or the realized outcome.

Some of the endogeneities can be characterized as cases of depletion: that is, the replication of success results, on average, in a lower performance because the replication itself is detrimental to subsequent outcomes. The most obvious cases involve resources that are depleted by use or competition. Other cases involve the corrosion of advantage through exploiting it (Barnett and Hansen 1996). Suppose, for example, that a tennis player follows a strategy of hitting the ball to the weaker side of his or her opponents, thus increasing the short-run prospects of victory but at the same time providing more practice for opponents in using their weaker hands than in using the stronger. Over time, practice effects will reduce the differences in competence between the two hands of competitors and thus reduce the competitive advantage of hitting to the weaker side. Other examples include cases of boredom or cynicism. Still others involve the adjustments of others, as for example when crying wolf changes the longer-run likelihood of a response to the cry.

Of possibly even greater importance, however, are cases involving outcome distributions that are augmented by use—where the replication itself improves the outcome distribution. An important case involves the effect of practice on performance. Each time a given alternative is chosen, its capability improves. It seems reasonable to assume that, typically, the effect of practice is to increase the mean and decrease the variance of the outcome distribution for the chosen alternative.

Practice effects complicate the use of success replication in finding an optimum choice. This complication is usually described in terms of "competency traps" (Levitt and March 1988; Arthur 1989). Suppose performance in a particular activity is a product of a fixed potential for the activity and a variable level of competence at it. Competence is characteristically low initially but increases through practice. Since performance reflects the product of competence and potential, practice effects make identification of the alternative with the highest potential more difficult than it would be in the absence of practice effects. It is quite possible that an alternative of lower potential will come to dominate one of greater potential by virtue of greater current competence on the former. This is particularly likely when comparing an existing inferior alternative at which an organization has a prolonged history of practice with a new superior alternative with which the organization is relatively inexperienced. Replication of success is more likely to aggravate this problem than to ameliorate it.

Similarly, if success makes subsequent success more likely, as in the "Matthew Effect" (Merton 1968), outcome distributions are endogenous to choices. Suppose, for example, that realized performance at time t, r_t, is a draw from a normal distribution with mean=x_t and standard deviation=s_t. If x_t is a function of r_{t-1} (for example, $x_t = r_{t-1}$) the process takes on martingale characteristics, with the result that small initial differences among alternatives are converted, over time, into large differences. An obvious organizational example is the way in which evaluations of early performance influence evaluations of subsequent performance so that small initial variability in evaluations of personnel becomes large variability. A related example is found in the way that the likelihood of imitation of a particular practice depends on its "legitimacy," which in turn depends on the number of others who have already adopted the practice (Carroll and Hannan 1989; Hannan 1998).

The replication of success is also affected by the definition of success in terms of a relation to aspirations and the ways in which aspirations are affected by achievements (Payne, Laughhann, and Crum 1980, 1981). Suppose the aspiration level at time t is a mix between aspiration at t−1 and performance at t−1. Thus, aspiration tends to track performance (is, in fact, an exponentially weighted moving average of performance) and essentially discounts current performance by a positive function of past performance. This makes subjective success or subjective failure particularly sensitive to noise in outcome determination. By making success (and thus the replications of success) depend on the history of past performances, adaptive aspirations tend to slow learning, especially if the rate of aspiration adjustment is rapid (March and Shapira 1992). On the other hand, if aspirations do not adjust to experience, so that success or failure tends to be stable, learning can become superstitious (Lave and March 1975).

Thus there are three simultaneous elements of learning. The first is *learning what to do:* looking for a good (or best) alternative technology, strategy, partner, etc. The second is *learning how to do it:* refining and improving competence with an alternative. The third is *learning what to hope for:* modifying the aspiration level for performance. The simultaneous adaptation of these three elements complicates the effectiveness of locating the best alternative. Adaptiveness in making a technology work and adaptiveness in aspirations interfere with adaptiveness in choosing a superior technology.

Fourth, sampling rates of experience are affected by sample outcomes. Experience in a particular time period can be seen as a draw from the distribution of possible outcomes associated with an alternative. Any particular experience is likely to be misleading to the extent to which there is variation in possible outcomes; and small samples of experience will have greater sampling error than will larger samples. The repetition of alternatives associated with success and the avoidance of alternatives associated with failure assure that the sample size of experience with successful alternatives will be larger than the sample size of experience with unsuccessful alternatives. As a result, the sampling error associated with unsuccessful alternatives will be larger than the sampling error associated with successful alternatives.

Two types of errors in experiential learning stem from sampling errors. The first is the error produced when a sample of experience has unrepresentative high returns. The second is the error produced when a sample of experience has unrepresentative low returns. Since the sample size of successful alternatives is increased by the repetition of success, the errors made by overestimating the value of an alternative tend to be self-correcting. Repetition reduces the sampling error associated with experience with a successful alternative, thus exposing errors of overestimation. On the other hand, errors made by underestimating the value of an alternative are not self-correcting. Alternatives that are better than their early results will tend to be persistently underrated and underchosen.

Some of the phenomena can be illustrated by a simple model, as long as it is recognized to be a very stylized representation. Suppose a choice is made each time period among a set of fifty alternatives. Each alternative (A_i) is characterized by a normal outcome distribution with a mean=x_i and a standard deviation=s. The x_i's and s are fixed over time. The x_i's are themselves draws from a normal distribution with a mean=0 and a standard distribution=S. Each alternative has an initial reputation, $R_{i,0}=0$, the mean expectation within the population of alternatives. Subsequently, the value of $R_{i,t}$ for each chosen alternative equals the mean realization associated with a choice of that alternative. Thus, reputations at t may be based on as few as zero observations or as many as $t-1$. Each time period the alternative with the highest reputation, max $R_{i,t}$, is chosen and an outcome realized (a draw from the distribution for that alternative).

The properties of this simple model illustrate the consequences of the endogenous sampling rate. *Improvement:* When the alternatives have different means ($S>0$), the replication of success improves performance over time. Better alternatives are discovered and replicated. *Stability:* There is a strong tendency for the replication of success to become very stable in its choice of alternatives. This result occurs, though with less force, even when there are no differences among the alternatives ($S=0$). *Reputation error:* The difference between the reputation of the chosen alternative and the true mean of the outcome distribution for that alternative ($R_{i,t}-x_i$) is positive—that is, reputations of chosen alternatives overestimate capabilities. The error is large initially but declines over time, ultimately (after a very large number of periods) approaching zero. *Optimality:* If we compute the ratio between the mean of the chosen alternative and the mean of the best possible alternative among the fifty alternatives where $S>0$, the mean fraction of the optimum that the process realizes increases over time, but it falls far short of 1.0. The process rarely discovers the optimum.

A mixed story. The result is a mixed story. In simple situations where the causal structure is not complicated, replication of success frequently leads to improvement in performance over time if there are differences among the alternatives, their outcomes are relatively reliable (low variance), and an adequate sample of experience is obtained. Replication of success usually leads to stability, a steady increase in the likelihood of repeating a choice. It usually leads to improved reputation (past performance) of chosen alternatives for an extended period. Part of the improvement in reputation is due to the likelihood of choosing a better alternative, but part of it is due to selection of positive sampling error.

On the other hand, learning through the replication of success has troubling unfavorable properties. Even in simple situations, the choices made through replication of success are very likely to be substantially suboptimal. The replication of success at one level of learning confounds the replication of success at another level, producing, for example, competency traps. Even though the deviation of average performance from the expected value of the alternative ultimately approaches zero, for an extended period the realized performance of the chosen alternative reflects a substantial overestimation of that alternative's potential. Even when there are no differences among the alternatives (and thus nothing to learn in terms of having a preference among them), replication of success usually leads to increased stability of choice. The subjective sense of learning is likely to be profound even when there is nothing to be learned.

A striking feature of these results is the extent to which they depend less on attributes of the learner than on attributes of experience. When experience unfolds in a way that makes learning effective, intelligence is augmented by the replication of success. But when experience is organized, as it often is, by complexity, ambiguity, stochastic variability, and limited sample sizes, the replication of success—whether through trial-and-error learning, imitation, or selection—is likely to lead to suboptimal outcomes.

LOW-INTELLECT LEARNING AND HIGH-INTELLECT EXPLANATIONS

Although it is flawed in important ways, replication of success is a ubiquitous instrument of learning. In one form or another, and despite its substantial disabilities, it characterizes much of the adaptiveness of human actors. At the same time, however, the low-intellect simplicities of trial-and-error learning, imitation, and selection conflict with high-intellect hopes. Human conceit (both among actors and among observers) often seems to eschew attributions of human behavior to success replication in favor of more complicated, cognitive comprehensions, explanations, and justifications.

The joint ubiquity of success replication and of preferences for high-intellect explications of history and learning suggests the possibility that behavior that is commonly described in high-intellect terms actually may reflect rules learned through low-intellect replications of actions associated with success. It is an old idea, much beloved by Pavlovians and behavioral psychologists and (in a different form) by economic theorists.

Suppose the mechanisms of human behavior are actually much less complicated than the interpretations humans make of human behavior. In particular, suppose it were possible to show that important elements of observed behavior are "explainable" as products of simple success replication. Such a demonstration would hardly prove that success replication is the primary mechanism producing the observed behavior, but it might invite some skepticism toward more elaborate explanations. To illustrate, consider two familiar areas of human inquiry into human behavior: the taking of risks and the choosing of mates.

Risk Taking

The most common observation (assumption) about risk-taking behavior is that human beings have different risk traits, some of them being risk averse, some risk-seeking. Generally it is assumed that most humans are risk averse. For example, they tend to prefer a certain reward of k dollars to a lottery that offers a probability, p, of receiving k/p dollars and $(1-p)$ of receiving nothing, although the expected value of either alternative is k.

A standard explanation of risk aversion for money is the presumed decreasing marginal utility of money so that the expected utility of a certain alternative is greater than that of a lottery with an equivalent monetary expectation. More generally, in classical theories of rational choice, "risk preference" is defined simply as any nonlinearity in the utility for money.

Studies of risk-taking behavior have suggested that risk taking is not so much an individual trait or a nonlinearity in utility as it is context dependent. The most common characterization is that with respect to alternatives whose expected returns exceed an aspiration level ("gains"), individuals tend to be risk averse, but with respect to alternatives whose expected returns lie below an aspiration level ("losses"), they tend to be risk-seeking (Kahneman and Tversky 1979). This has sometimes been given a "satisficing" interpretation (March and Shapira 1992).

Suppose that risk preference is neither a trait nor immediately context dependent but is the result of learning. It has been shown that simple success replication learning will lead to risk aversion for gains and risk seeking for losses (March 1999c, chap. 15; Denrell 2007). The possible advantages to be reaped from high-variance alternatives in the gains area are poorly assessed by small samples, and those alternatives tend to be abandoned on the basis of poor small sample results. In the loss area, on the other hand, negative results from the low-variance alternatives induce sampling of the high-variance ones.

An important special case of this phenomenon involves learning in cases having very low-probability, extreme outcomes. Very low-probability events result in a highly skewed distribution of the number of occurrences. For example, what happens with respect to a major scientific breakthrough in a laboratory? Such an event is extremely positive, but the chance of its occurring is very small. Most researchers in a laboratory will never experience such an event. In effect (or possibly in fact), most learners will underestimate the likelihood of an extremely rare, positive event. Their resulting actions will be implicitly risk averse, and researchers will fail to replicate the behaviors (e.g., intense commitment and involvement) associated with a great scientific discovery as often as might be justified.

Alternatively, consider what happens in cases involving low-probability, extremely negative consequences. An example would be nuclear accidents in a nuclear power plant. The likelihood is extremely low, so most operators in a nuclear power plant do not experience the event. In effect (or possibly in fact) most learners will underestimate the likelihood of an extremely rare, negative event. Their resulting actions will be implicitly risk-seeking, and they will replicate behaviors (e.g., carelessness) that increase the likelihood of a nuclear accident's occurring. In such cases, risk aversion for gains and risk seeking for losses would be produced simply by learning.

Notice the difference between the two cases. In the case of the rare, positive event, the failure to experience the event induces individuals to avoid repeating actions (e.g., working diligently on the project) that would make the positive event more likely, thereby not only *reducing* the chance of correcting the implicit underestimation of its likelihood but also actually making its occurrence *less* likely. Learning reduces the chance of a major scientific breakthrough. In the case of the rare, negative event, the failure to experience the event induces individuals to repeat actions (e.g., sloppiness, inattention) that make the negative event more likely, thereby not only *increasing* the chance of correcting the implicit underestimation of its likelihood but also actually making its occurrence *more* likely. Learning increases the chance of a major nuclear accident, "correcting" the underestimation of the risk both by greater experience with it and by making its occurrence more likely.

In this respect, Beverly Sauer, after reviewing experience with regulations in hazardous environments, observes, "Agencies write standards because experience is a poor teacher" (2003, 37). Sauer explains that constant exposure to danger without its realization leaves human beings less concerned about what once terrified them, and therefore experience can have the paradoxical effect of having people learn to feel more immune than they should to the unlikely dangers that surround them.

Mate Choosing

Consider a world in which a person experiences and records each performance of a candidate for selection as a mate. To simplify, assume the candidates, on their part, make no choices but are simply available to be chosen. Each candidate's performance is a draw from a normal distribution of possible performances. A candidate is chosen each time period by evaluating past experience with all candidates, recording the average performance of each candidate previously chosen, and anticipating that candidates who have not been chosen previously will, on average, have a performance equal to the mean of those who have.

What will be the key properties of such a world of mate seekers who learn from experience by replicating successes? Three properties of interest may be worth noting:

(1) The likelihood that a mate chosen in this way will be the best possible mate is small.
(2) The process will yield monogamy; that is, the choices made in one time period will tend increasingly to be repeated in the next. That tendency to monogamy will be moderated by postdecision disappointment but accentuated by competency gains from experience in the relationship.
(3) Participants in the process will understand themselves as having learned from experience successfully and will have confidence in their choices.

Thus we are led, perhaps, to what might be called the behaviorist manifesto. Risk aversion is not necessarily to be seen as a thoughtful choice, a mysterious trait, or a consequence of context; it can be pictured as a propensity produced by simple learning from ordinary experience. Monogamy is not necessarily produced by cultural norms or morality or by calculated rationality; it can be seen as a consequence of simple learning from ordinary experience.

It is not necessary to embrace entirely such skepticism about the more elaborate stories and theories articulated by scholars. The more elaborate stories may, in fact, be true even though particular aspects of the behavior can be approximated by a simple replication hypothesis. In both cases, however, the more complex interpretations by human actors and by economists, philosophers, psychologists, sociologists, and theologians can be seen as possibly reflecting elements of human conceit about the role of human intention and intellect in human behavior. They can be seen as stories told to honor and reinforce that conceit, a purpose possibly as noble as reflecting truth but different from it.

3

LEARNING THROUGH STORIES AND MODELS

Organizations pursue intelligence through the low-intellect adaptive processes discussed in chapter 2. They also use high-intellect processes, which are the focus of this chapter. Low-intellect processes operate by replicating actions associated with experienced success. High-intellect processes operate by devising explicit understandings that fit the events of experience into a causal explanation through a natural language narrative, an analytical model, or a theory. High-intellect stories and models are bases both for refined understanding and appreciation of history and for differentiating among humans with respect to their knowledge.

Narratives of experience fill many studies of organizations, biographies and autobiographies of managers, journalist reports of organizational events, and the daily recitations of participants making sense of the events of organizational history. These narratives explore the events of episodes of history in order to discern the causal antecedents of experience.

Similarly, models of experience fill many studies of organizations and the teachings of universities and consultants. Decision theory, economic theory, organization theory, game theory, and the stories told within those frames are centerpieces of organizational intelligence.

For some decades after the Second World War, stories and models generated by high-intellect processes for improving intelligence enjoyed a period of exceptional approbation. Although the fervor of the approval subsequently suffered from several conspicuous failures—most notably the defeat of the "best and the brightest" of the United States in Vietnam, the collapse of a monument to rational planning, the Soviet Union, and the orgies of disappointments with complicated strategies, hedge funds, and derivatives in financial markets—these stories and models of organizational life became almost taken for granted. They sustained a large collection of academics, writers, consultants, and practitioners.

High-intellect stories and models reflect the joint effects of two pressures. On the one hand, there is pressure that a story or model honor intelligence with subtlety and complexity that make it interesting. On the other hand, there is pressure that a story or model be simple enough to be comprehensible. The joint effect is a tendency for stories and models to be elaborate enough to celebrate human intellect but no more elaborate than their audience can tolerate. They tend to exhibit what might be called maximum comprehensible complexity.

Maximum comprehensible complexity is itself a function of the intelligence of audiences and the technology of stories and models, so it varies from one audience to another, from one instrument of storytelling to another, and over time. However, it is relatively insensitive to the underlying complexity of the process being described. Insofar as stories and models reflect maximum comprehensible complexity, they tend to be systematically more complex than simple processes and simpler than complex processes. The former tendency was explored briefly in chapter 2; the latter tendency is examined in this chapter.

STORIES AND MODELS

From the great Norse skalds (Sturluson 1984) to modern journalists (Halberstam 1972), humans have been inveterate storytellers. Roland Barthes (1977) describes narratives as universal, and Barbara Czarniawska (1997, 28) observes that interview respondents want to tell stories rather than answer questions. Managers, journalists, and scholars create and share stories and models of experience as bases for describing, explaining, and improving the events of organizational life and for establishing reputations for personal acumen. The objectives, techniques, and problems of such efforts are common among scholars, journalists, management consultants, and organizational participants. They are all storytellers and model builders (Weick 1995).

Stories and models are responses to an urge that permeates organizational life and organizations research. It is the urge to describe the causal basis of experience. Experience consists in a stream of events produced by processes that are complex, stochastic, and only partly observable. Causality is ambiguous. Generating an explanation of history involves transforming the ambiguities and complexities of experience into a form that is elaborate enough to elicit interest, simple enough to be understood, and credible enough to be accepted. The art of storytelling involves a delicate balancing of those three criteria.

Some features of human cognitive abilities and styles affect the ways stories and models are created from ambiguous and complex experience. Humans have limited capabilities to store and recall history. They are sensitive to reconstructed memories that serve current beliefs and desires. They have limited capabilities for analysis, a limitation that makes them sensitive to the framing that is given to experience. They conserve belief by being less critical of evidence that seems to confirm prior beliefs than of evidence that seems to disconfirm them. They distort both observations and beliefs in order to make them consistent. They prefer simple causalities, ideas that place causes and effects close to one another and that match big effects with big causes. They prefer heuristics that involve limited information and simple calculations to more complex analyses. This general picture of human interpretations of experience is well documented and well known (Camerer, Loewenstein, and Rabin 2004; Kosnik 2008).

These elements of individual human storytelling are embedded in the interconnected, coevolutionary feature of social interpretation. An individual learns from many others who are simultaneously learning from him or her and from each other. The stories and theories that one individual embraces are not independent of the stories and theories held by others. Since learning responds as a result to echoes of echoes, ordinary life almost certainly provides greater consistency of observations and interpretations of them than is justified by the underlying reality. In particular, ordinary life generally seems to lead to greater confirmation of prior understandings than is probably warranted.

Explanation fits experienced events into accepted frames. In economics, explanation involves demonstrating that observed events are consistent with the accepted axioms of rationality. In physics, explanation involves demonstrating that observed events are consistent with accepted physical laws. In fundamentalist religions, explanation involves demonstrating that observed events are consistent with accepted scripture. The key effort is to link experience with a preexistent accepted story line so as to achieve a subjective sense of understanding.

There are contending frames, of course, and the process of fitting experience into them involves negotiation over their comparative interest, comprehensibility, and credibility. The terms of such negotiation, particularly the relation between credibility and empirical validation, are the topics of treatises on scientific method and debates among scholars. Contestation over validity exhibits differences among scholars, but it typically depends on some level of shared recognition of a basic frame. Where such agreement is lacking, discussions of the interest, comprehensibility, and credibility of explanations can be acrimonious and incoherent. Experience interpreted within a Marxist frame is mostly unintelligible to a neoclassical economist. Experience interpreted within a Freudian frame is mostly unintelligible to a behavioral psychologist. And experience interpreted within a Foucauldian frame is mostly unintelligible to an organizational population ecologist.

The most obvious difference among storytellers of organizational experience is between those who see knowledge as expressed in natural language organized into narrative simplifications (roughly the literary/humanistic tradition) and those who see knowledge as expressed in abstract concepts organized into symbolic simplifications (roughly the mathematical/scientific tradition) (Snow 1959). Within the natural language contingent, the emphasis is on themes and grammars, and life is seen as represented by a narrative with conventions of texts. Within the symbolic language contingent, the emphasis is on the choice of mathematical frame, assumptions, and derivations, and life is seen as represented by a model with conventions of mathematical logic and formal rules of proof and inference.

Organizational storytellers, model builders, and theorists seek to make their interpretations both realistic and comprehensible, but the two objectives are inconsistent (Lévi-Strauss 1966, 261; Augier and March 2008, 96–98). Experience is rooted in a complicated causal system that can be described adequately only by a description that is too complex for the human mind. The more accurately reality is reflected, the less comprehensible the story, and the more comprehensible the story, the less realistic it is. The richness of life is made comprehensible only by creating portrayals of life that are, of necessity, incomplete. As Nietzsche (1997, 279) wrote: "Partial knowledge is more often victorious than full knowledge: it conceives things as simpler than they are and therefore makes its opinion easier to grasp and more persuasive."

Stories and models simplify complex causal relations, reducing the number of variables involved, often ignoring second- and third-order effects, minimizing feedback effects, and glossing over variations in time delays. They often result in overfitting, explanations that provide *post hoc* interpretations of random variation that offer little subsequent predictive power. They simplify identities and the occasions for their evocation, reducing the nuance of identity fulfillment and the chaos of human obligations. They generally assume that causal stories are decomposable into simple subtexts that do not involve detailed interaction with each other. These simplifications necessarily reflect incomplete representations, but they facilitate comprehension. The models and stories of experience have to be in a form that can be communicated and understood.

The practitioners of natural language intelligence work endlessly through cycles of resolution and doubt, glorying in dilemmas, contradictions, and inconsistencies. Building on and venerating the indeterminacy of natural language, they interpret and reinterpret, less in a pursuit of closure than in a spirit of renewal (Ricoeur 1965; White 1987; Polkinghorne 1988; Czarniawska 1997; Gabriel 2004). The practitioners of analytical models similarly cycle between doubt and resolution but with a stronger conception of the possibility of progress toward the latter. They honor the openness and flexibilities of mathematics and statistics with their manifestations in imaginative extensions and systematic derivations. They see themselves as driven by a pursuit of extralinguistic truth (Kuhn 1962; Lave and March 1975; Williamson 1975; Scott 1981), but they find themselves persistently prone to statistical overfitting (Hastie, Tibshirani, and Friedman 2001).

In a manner quite similar to that of novelists and playwrights, managers, journalists, lawyers, and students of organizations eliminate and add facts to make a better (more compelling? more accurate?) story (Collingwood 1993). In the process, storytellers or model builders may reject some widely believed "facts" (e.g., miracles) as well as inject "facts" that are not observed but assumed (e.g., "constitutive imagination," "stylized facts").

They also fit experience into a recognizable story line. Barbara Czarniawska wrote, "Stories do not emerge out of thin air; a great deal of collective work of the kind that Weick (1995) called *sensemaking* goes into their construction. . . . When a new event occurs, . . . it is made meaningful by setting it in an existing frame, even if it may mean that the frame must be somewhat adjusted and changed" (2008, 33, 38). Events are assembled into culturally familiar story types about them. For example, lawyers and courts create stylized stories and interpretations and seek both to learn from them and to provide their frames as bases for interpretations of testimony (Bennett and Feldman 1981).

Stories and models are never the product of one person

alone. The storytellers have to deal not only with competing storytellers but also with the prejudices and expectations of listeners. They have to deal with participants who consciously seek to control interpretations by investing in authorized personal historians, called public relations experts or spin doctors. Storytellers have their individual sources and biases, but they have to gain acceptance of their stories by catering to their audiences. The primary way the themes underlying stories and models secure acceptance is through a social process of telling, retelling, reshaping, and evaluation by which interpretive ideas develop and diffuse through a population of storytellers and listeners involved in a common culture with a common language.

The idea that simplifications of experience within familiar frames are bases of human understanding and behavior is shared, though in somewhat different forms, by literary theorists (e.g., Ricoeur 1965), legal theorists (Dworkin 1986), phenomenologists (e.g., Schütz 1967; Berger and Luckmann 1967), symbolic interactionists (e.g., Blumer 1969; Van Maanen 1988, 1995), and ethnomethodologists (e.g., Garfinkel 1967; Cicourel 1974). The same processes of familiarization are evident in the development of formal models—for example, when the models of economics assume the easily comprehended form of models of physics (Mirowski 1989), or when complex systems of multiple variables are modeled as variations on linear regression (Greene 2008).

Thus, stories and models of experience are fictions seeking social confirmation as truth. They are fictions because truth is inaccessible. However, they represent a particular variety of fiction. They are fictions that explicitly invite confrontation with the evidence of observation, even while recognizing both the complexity of causality and the opaqueness of its observation. This tension between the aspirations for valid comprehensibility and the complexities and ambiguities of history permeates efforts to construct and confirm stories and models of experience. It also underlies challenges to the assumption that the simplifying heuristics of human cognition reflect regrettable irrationalities (Hogarth and Karelaia 2005; Gigerenzer and Brighton 2009).

Storytelling and model building also fuel the fundamental circularity of learning from experience. Humans are urged to learn from the experiences of history, but the experiences of history are encapsulated in frames invented by humans. Humans learn from their own inventions. The circularity does not preclude a meaningful augmentation of intelligence through exposure to experience, but it increases the possibilities for confusion and resistance to discrepant information in the process (Kuhn 1962).

THE STORIES OF ORGANIZATIONS

The world of organizations and management invites storytelling (Zaleznick 1989; Westerlund and Sjøstrand 1979; Gabriel 2004). Knowledge is sought about experience, but experience is ambiguous and its causal structure complex. Identities are ambiguous, and the ways in which they apply to particular situations are intricately multifaceted. The development and elaboration of stories and models of experience are a major part of the documentation of management. Participants are asked what happened and why it happened, and research often consists primarily in tabulating the stories told by storytellers (Sarbin 1986; White 1987; Collingwood 1993; Bruner 1996; Golden-Biddle and Locke 1997).

Stories of organizational experience are found in business cases taught in business schools and in administrative cases taught in public management programs. They are found in business plans discussed by venture capitalists and in discussions of administrative reform in government. They fill popular management books and the media. They are embedded in economic and organizational theories of choice. The storytellers of organizations are, for the most part, associated with the stock analyst, business press, political pundit, and academic trades. The ability to tell interesting, comprehensible, and credible stories is a mark of intelligence among observers of organizations.

The stories of organizations, like stories of many other parts of modern life, are told both in the guise of formal models and in the guise of narratives. Much of contemporary organizational economics assumes the form of a few simple equations (Gibbons and Roberts 2008) that can be used to provide economic interpretations of organizational regularities (Kreps 1990a). The ideas are abstractions representing elementary characteristics of organizational life that are used to interpret properties drawn from the elaborate details of that life. Much of the rest of contemporary literature reporting research on business firms or governmental agencies assumes a narrative form in which organizational experience is interpreted in terms of stories that extract a few themes from, or impose them on, the rich detail of organizational experience (Czarniawska 1997; Hernes 2008).

Often the stories are contested. Consider attempts to describe the rise of Microsoft and its human symbol, Bill Gates. In version 1 of the Microsoft story, Gates is pictured as a brilliant innovator and tactician with extraordinary insight and managerial ability. It is a variation on earlier stories of Andrew Carnegie and Henry Ford. In version 2 of the Microsoft story, Gates is pictured as a lucky bully who never had an original idea in his life but has been ruthless in stealing and promoting the ideas of others. It is a variation on the robber baron stories of the nineteenth century. One reason for the contestation is, of course, that the future of Microsoft and its competitors is itself contested. In the same way in which Americans are considerably more likely than non-Americans to attribute the rise to power of the United States to admirable properties of the nation and its citizens, positive stories of Microsoft are more characteristic of people who live in Seattle than of those who live in San José or Salt Lake City.

Some of the problems involved in high-intellect processes for experiential learning can be illustrated by efforts to convert the experiences of corporate history into an understanding of organizational profitability. Business firms sometimes do well, sometimes do poorly. Managers and researchers seek to use observed experience as a means for identifying attributes that differentiate high-performing (profitable) from low-performing (unprofitable) organizations.

They try to tell acceptable stories about the reasons for the pattern that is observed, a pattern that typically arises from a complex combination of actions taken by many individuals and organizations, as well as the vagaries of fate.

Although claims of knowledge about the determinants of organizational performance are a standard feature not only of popular do-it-yourself books but also of the research literature, it is hard to avoid the conclusion that (within the standards of inference that are accepted as conventional in science) most studies of organizational performance are unable to untangle the causal structure affecting performance with any confidence. The difficulties stem, in large part, from (a) the extent to which organizations have assimilated past understandings and thereby considerably reduced variability in policies, practices, and forms; (b) the mismatch between the complexities of the causal system and the simplicity of the ideas used to describe it; (c) the dependence of profit on factors that are unobservable or simultaneously codetermined by profit; (d) the large number of uncontrolled factors; and (e) the small sample size of experience. These difficulties in identifying the causal structure of organizational performance are neither secret nor recently discovered (Staw 1975; Lenz 1981; March and Sutton 1997). They are regularly noted in critical reviews and are taught in elementary courses in quantitative and qualitative inference.

Despite the complications in extracting reality from experience, or perhaps because of them, there is a tendency for the themes of stories of management to converge over time. Ideas about the determinants of profitability come to be shared as part of the story of "good practice." The interpretations of Bill Gates are likely to achieve some kind of shared understanding, as have the interpretations of Henry Ford and Genghis Khan. The shared understandings will not be based exclusively on accumulated evidence, although it will certainly accumulate. Rather, they will develop as conventions of discourse, as part of what it means to be an educated person and as part of establishing standing in ordinary conversations.

MYTHIC THEMES

Standard journals and books dealing with both the private and public sectors tell stories of organizational history that emphasize a few conventional themes. Included in those themes are some easily recognized ideas about experience. Outcomes are produced by people, and thus stories of people and events are intertwined. The world is one in which there is competition for primacy, and only the fittest survive. Problems have solutions, and those solutions can be found by intelligence. The world changes, and ability to adapt is necessary for survival. These stories and story themes are obviously vital to the ways in which people in organizations comprehend their histories. They form the bases of interpreting experience and the frames within which experience can be shared.

In particular, stories of organizational experience are deeply affected by themes that are accurately described as myths: "Any real or fictional story, recurring theme, or character type that appeals to the consciousness of a people by embodying its cultural ideals or by giving expression to deep, commonly felt emotions" (*The American Heritage Dictionary of the English Language* 1981).

Myths are instruments for reducing the confusions of experience, human comprehension, and human enactment. Stories or models with mythic standard story lines provide comprehensible meaning and credibility (Vygotsky [1962] 1986; White 1987). Mythic story lines are not straitjackets. They combine sacredness (and stability) with some openness to variation. Constructing stories from mythic themes involves many different stories and substories (mythemes in Lévi-Strauss's terms) that provide plenty of material for bricolage by storytellers (Lévi-Strauss 1966, 1979). The options are, however, limited by the necessity to construct a story that will be deemed credible, and credibility thrives on familiarity.

Organizational stories and models are built particularly around four main mythic themes (March 1999b). The first mythic theme is the myth of *rationality:* the idea that the human spirit finds definitive expression through taking and justifying action in terms of its future consequences for prior values. Action is understood as reflecting choice, and choice is seen as made in terms of consequences.

Rationality is seen as both a dictum of good behavior and a prediction of behavior. It is pervasive in the stories and models of both public and private management. It underlies the extensive discussions of "incentives" as critical to organizational behavior. It is the basis of answers to the question "why did you/he/she/they/I/we do that?" The answer is given in terms of expectations of consequences and incentives: the action was taken because it made consequential sense. In the conventions of economics as those conventions have become folk wisdom, behavior is explained when a rational consequential reason can be given for it.

The second mythic theme is the myth of *hierarchy:* the idea that problems and actions can be decomposed into nested sets of subproblems and subactions such that interactions among them can be organized within a hierarchy. Hierarchical decomposition is the basis for the hierarchical organization of problem solving and organization. It involves a combination of decentralized (in parallel) work and integration, with integration being hierarchical. Responsibility for accomplishing a complex task can be arranged in a system of subordination and domination in which each higher level controls and integrates the solutions and actions at a lower level. Ideas about hierarchically organized control and accountability permeate organizational stories. They are reflected in organization charts and business plans. They are the basis for efforts to allocate personal responsibility for success and failure and for a host of standard prescriptions for effective organizational structures.

The myth of hierarchy suppresses the possible importance of other kinds of network structures. For example, the symmetry of the story of game theory with its coalitions among parallel actors is transformed in discussions of organizations into a story of hierarchically dominant "principals" who achieve their objectives through clever management of incentives offered to subordinate "agents" (Milgrom and Roberts 1992). The intricacy of informal networks and their importance are subordinated to the formal hierarchy of an organization.

The third mythic theme is the myth of *individual leader significance:* the idea that any story of history must be related to a human project in order to be meaningful and that organizational history is produced by the intentions of specific human leaders. In typical organizational stories or models, individual actions are presumed to be the basic building blocks for understanding organizational experience. Events of history are seen as due to human intentions and as produced by the interaction of identifiable individual projects of competition and cooperation (Polkinghorne 1988). Major developments in organizational history are imagined to be attributable to exceptional human action and capabilities, that is, to the actions of leaders.

Managerial/organizational history is as filled with heroes as is military history, from which it takes many of its metaphors (Kieser 1997). A fascination with the rise and fall of companies is translated into stories of the rise and fall of leaders. Just as stories of the rise and fall of armies become stories of the competence and incompetence of generals, stories of the growth and decline of business firms become stories of the vision and lack of it of CEOs. The identity, character, and obligations of leadership are common foci for managerial education.

The fourth mythic theme is the myth of *historical effi-*

ciency: the idea that history follows a path leading to a unique equilibrium defined by antecedent conditions and produced by competition. The theme is an essential basis for the emphasis on market competition as a selective mechanism among business organizations. The basic ideas are that history favors those individuals, organizations, forms, practices, and beliefs that match the requirements of their environments; that efficiency is assured through competition; and that survival is evidence of superior fit to environmental requirements. Historical efficiency is an elementary idea borrowed from classical functionalism as supplemented by Malthus ([1798] 2001) and Darwin ([1859] 2006). Competitive outcomes are seen as necessary in an environment; victories result from superiorities; defeats result from deficiencies.

Historical efficiency appears in stories of the triumph of good organizational practices (e.g., quality circles, new public management, lean production, business process reengineering, total quality management, organizational culture, knowledge management) over inferior practices. It appears in the inclination to treat the results of market or political competition as natural and necessary. Patently, there is a certain inconsistency between the myth of individual leader significance and the myth of historical efficiency, but the combination of familiar but inconsistent themes is a common feature of human storytelling.

The four myths are by no means an exhaustive listing of the themes available to organizational storytellers. There are many others of varying consistency with them and of varying acceptability. In particular, each of the main themes has a countertheme that is well enough known to qualify as a possible element in a story. The countertheme to the myth of rationality is the theme of identity. Rather than following a logic of consequences, individuals match situations to the demands of an identity. The countertheme to the myth of hierarchy is the theme of nonhierarchical networks. Individuals are joined in complicated networks of associations. The countertheme to the myth of individual leader significance is the theme of complexity. History is made by the actions of complex combinations of many individuals. The countertheme to the myth of historical efficiency is the theme of historical inefficiency. The processes of adaptation are slow and have multiple equilibria.

Stories built on the main myths undoubtedly will more easily find credence than will stories built on the counterthemes, but part of the process of mythic development is found in the experiments with themes by storytellers. They provide opportunities to elaborate the main myths to accommodate new refinements and to test the possibilities for fundamental reorientation of the mythic basis of stories. At the same time, the way in which counterthemes are positioned as denials of the primary themes tends to highlight the central intellectual position of the latter.

Underlying many of these myths is a grand myth of human significance: the idea that humans can, through their individual and collective intelligent actions, influence the course of history to their advantage. Such a myth is both a matter of faith and a basis for interpretations of experience. It is widely accepted as obvious, though it is clearly more widely believed in successful organizations and cultures than in those where success is less familiar. It is not self-evident—or perhaps only that.

The myth of human significance produces the cruelties and generosities stemming from the human inclination to assign credit and blame for events to human intention. Responsibility for social and economic well-being is allocated to political parties and politicians. Responsibility for profits and losses and for changes in stock value is allocated to managers of firms. Responsibility for public satisfaction or dissatisfaction with social programs is allocated to political leaders or to managers of governmental agencies, creating "adequately blameworthy" agents (Shklar 1990, 62). In the course of such allocation of responsibility, any possible distinction between personal moral responsibility as a confirmation of human significance and behavioral responsibility as an assertion of causality tends to be lost. As Robert Reich (1985, 23–28) observes, "There is an overwhelming tendency in American life to lionize or pillory the people who stand at the helms of our large institutions—to offer praise or level blame for outcomes over which they may have little control." These certifications of human control over destiny are precious to human ideology (Czarniawska 1997, 38–39). On a more mundane level, the myth of accountability that they sustain affects managerial behavior in observable ways (Tetlock 1992).

TRUTH, JUSTICE, AND BEAUTY

Stories and models of experience comprise a large fraction of the effort to learn from experience by educated observers of organization. They find their primary traditional value in their claim to being accurate representations of an extralinguistic truth, but they also find value in their contributions to justice—creating social order—and beauty—the aesthetic pleasure they provide.

Truth Value

Within conventional interpretations, intelligent action demands accurate comprehension of the world, and an accurate comprehension of the world demands an accurate interpretation of experience. Insofar as the themes on which the stories of experience are built either correctly portray the world or create the world, the stories will provide useful guides for action. Words such as "reality," "accurate interpretation," and "correct portrayal" are anathema to purists of social construction, but for most people they have patent relevance to a discussion of learning.

Although it is widely believed that organizations or scholars can, in principle, develop stories and models that correctly represent the underlying reality of organizational life (Argyris and Schön 1978; Nonaka and Takeuchi 1995), the procedures by which stories and models are created, in themselves, offer few guarantees of validity. This is not primarily because human learners are incompetent. The reality they are asked to reflect is difficult to discern in ordinary experience, even with the best tools of observation and inference. The world is too complex and experience is too meager. For example, business school students are trained to take events of simulated experience in business cases and interpret them according to the frames they have been provided, primarily from economics but on other occasions from organization studies, accounting, operations research, marketing, or other domains. The exercise may well be useful, but it would be hard to claim that the interpretive stories they tell are unambiguously implicit in the events.

Similarly, stories interpreting observed experience are among the earlier and more respected contributions to research in organization studies. Examples include studies by Abegglen (1958) of the Japanese factory, Gouldner (1954) of industrial bureaucracy, Roethlisberger and Dickson (1939) and Walker and Guest (1952) of worker groups, Whyte (1955) of street corner organization, Selznick (1949) of cooptation, and Kaufman (1960) of the forest ranger. These studies, as well as many others like them, have been very important sources of ideas for students of organizations, although it is hard to view the ideas presented as unambiguously implicit in the events described in the studies. Indeed, some of the more artful practitioners of the craft resist making their own explicit interpretations, leaving meanings to be elaborated by others (Chekhov 1979; Krieger 1979).

Stories from experience are often profoundly believed and widely shared, but neither the depth of beliefs nor the generality of agreement about them speaks decisively to their validity. Moreover, the comprehension of experience is often contested. Widely shared beliefs are widely challenged. Contemporaries argue about what happened and why it happened. Beliefs about the lessons of experience are often localized by political or linguistic boundaries. Colonial history is told differently in different places. Individuals write memoirs and autobiographies, seeking to affect interpretations of the events of history, but they do not agree among themselves. As is often observed, history is written by the winners. In particular, history as recorded is a story told to (and by) victorious leaders. As a result, it is usually a story of the actions and intentions of leaders and mirrors the properties of skaldic histories of glorious heroes.

Although conventionalized understandings often endure for extended periods, any portrayal of historical interpretation as stable over time is inconsistent with the history of history. Beliefs about historical experience change gradually, partly in response to new information and partly in response to new interpretive ideas. As the prejudices of dominant groups change, the stories of history reflect changing political correctness: Puritan rigidities change from symbols of steadfastness to symbols of bigotry. Native Americans change from savages to environmental pioneers.

In his famous parable about the emperor's new clothes, Hans Christian Andersen (1837) reminds his readers of the extent to which the social conception of reality may deviate from palpable truth. The story of the emperor's clothes, however, is potentially misleading. The storyteller reveals explicitly that the emperor is, in fact, naked. He invites his readers to see the ludicrous way in which social validation of a palpable falsehood is sustained until challenged by an innocent, not fully socialized boy. Thus, the readers of the story know the truth and see the errors of social consensus and conformity.

In the more typical case in real life, the truth is obscure. What is known is that almost everyone agrees that something is true, even though it may not seem to be true to a particular individual. This latter situation is considerably more problematic than the former. Confronted with consensus beliefs that the world is round, what are we to make of our own experience that seems to indicate it is flat? Confronted with consensus beliefs that smoking tobacco has adverse long-run effects, what are we to make of our own experience that smoking seems to make us feel better?

Much as the plots of acceptable romantic comedies can be specified by a student of films, the frames of most stories could probably be written without any knowledge of the specific events to be described. Indeed, part of the argument for stories and models is that the enduring frames on which they are based are closer to the truth than any particular set of contemporary observations. Is it possible that the story frames and models that we accept present truer pictures of reality than our direct experience? Giambattista Vico ([1725] 1961; Bitney 1969) argued that myths capture the essential elements of history, removing the irrelevant noise of actual events. In a similar way, it has been argued that a meta-analysis of numerous incomplete and erroneous stories of the rise of Nokia can be made to yield a valid story (Lamberg, Laukia, and Ojala 2008). And Kathryn March reported that the stories told by Tamang women about the experiences of their lives "are epics because what they tell is larger than any one telling, larger even than the sum of all possible tellings. They reach beyond themselves, full of connections apparently outside of, but in the end an integral part of, the stories" (2002, 12).

Likewise, a student of economics is assured that although immediate direct experience may sometimes seem to disconfirm the teachings of economic models, the problem is more likely to lie with the observations or their interpretations than with the theory.

The claims are powerfully instructive, and they evoke childhood memories of treating the poor results of classroom physics experiments as evidence of incompetent experimental techniques rather than erroneous theories. However, the claims are difficult either to validate empirically or to derive from widely believed assumptions. The argument suggests a kind of "central limit theorem" in which the random noise that confuses the interpretation of immediate experience is reduced by the pooling of experience reflected in the accepted frames of stylized stories. The number and credibility of assumptions required to justify the derivation are, however, daunting.

On the surface, at least, it appears that, outside closely constrained domains involving repeated experience, ordinary experience (observation) will not yield much in the way of unambiguously valid lessons if we apply the standards of evidence that are shared widely among scholars.

Anton Chekhov in a letter to his publisher, A. S. Suvorin, on May 30, 1888, wrote,

> It is time for writers, and particularly for artists, to admit that you can't figure out anything in this world, as Socrates once admitted and as Voltaire kept admitting. The public thinks it knows and understands everything; and the dumber it is the broader its horizons seem to be. However, if an artist whom the public believes decides to state that he understands nothing of what he sees, that in itself is of great significance in the realm of thought and is a great step forward. (Chekhov 1979, 270)

A similar kind of humility has been suggested for statistical model builders. The more general the model (i.e., the more alternative patterns of relationships and functional forms it allows), the greater the likelihood that the model will, in effect, "fit" the noise in the system, resulting in a good fit but poor predictability. This bias-variance dilemma (Geman, Bienenstock and Doursat 1992; Gigerenzer and Brighton 2009) forces a choice between the overfitting errors of complex models and the oversimplicity of simple ones.

Humility on the part of high-intellect learners and skepticism about the lessons they propose seem clearly warranted, but is there some alternative? Is it possible to justify as anything other than a personal or social prejudice our intuitive acceptance of some stories and rejection of others as containing germs of truth? By what criteria do we (or ought we to) judge one story as more credible than another? The plays of writers such as William Shakespeare, Henrik Ibsen, or Anton Chekhov are often portrayed as revealing important truths about the human condition and human behavior (O'Connor 2008). Indeed, they are sometimes used to instruct managers or those who aspire to be managers (Gagliardi and Czarniawska 2006). For example, Ibsen's plays have been used to develop the idea that powerful ideals suborn lies and to argue that such a mechanism operates in contemporary organizations (March 2008, chap. 20). The poetry of William Yeats has been used to explicate the managerial dilemma of speaking a rhetoric of decisiveness, certainty, and clarity while experiencing a life of doubt, paradox, and contradiction (March 2008, chap. 19). The theorems of game theory and the metaphors of garbage cans have been used to interpret the strategic behavior of business firms (Gibbons 1992; 2003). What does it mean to say that such observations resonate with our understandings and thereby deserve credence? How do we judge whether they are true?

Novelists, playwrights, artists, and social scientists all claim veracity in their stories and models, a link to widely shared understandings of the nature of experience. Some would say that what distinguishes the two groups is a difference in the willingness to see their specific stories or models as part of an explicitly collective endeavor to discover truth (Kuhn 1962) and thus, in principle, as disconfirmable through evidence. The difference is important, but it does not change a fundamental similarity. The stories of novelists and social scientists are judged, in part, on whether they are credible, and it seems unlikely that the assessment of credibility is enormously different in the two cases.

How do we assess the credibility of stories told by Chekhov? Is it different from the way we assess the credibility of stories told by Weick? Is credibility distinct from artistry? From technique? What are data of experience and how do they enter the calibration of credibility? Can credibility be separated from interest and ideology? Or from familiarity? The point is not to pretend to settle such issues. They seem to endure comfortably in the face of innumerable efforts to resolve them. The point is to observe that there is by no means general agreement that the stories and models of organization studies are more (or less) credible than the stories of novelists or playwrights.

In order to develop a technology for assessing credibility of stories and models, it will probably be necessary to recognize explicitly the tenuous link between experience and reality. When Carlos Fuentes (e.g., in *Aura*), Gabriel García Márquez (e.g., in *100 Years of Solitude*), or Isabel Allende (e.g., in *Stories of Eva Luna*) writes of worlds in which reality and fantasy are difficult to distinguish, each speaks not only for novelists but also for social scientists. The best of both breeds seeks to exhibit veracity and do so by methods in which imagination is often given an importance comparable to observation in capturing an elusive reality.

The possibility of extracting more information about an underlying reality from small, rich samples motivates modern work on "hypothetical histories." Such histories require the use of observed experience and imagination to generate distributions of possible experiences. In the process, possibilities derived from speculation are promoted to approximately the same status as observed reality (Tetlock 1999). It is a tempting direction, but it is difficult to provide persuasive demonstration of its validity or definitive elaboration of a standardized methodology to accomplish it.

Justice

The truth value of stories and models seems difficult to establish, but the stories told about experience are not simply instruments of causal truth. The myths and themes that frame experience are entrenched in, and at the same time contribute to, the development of taken-for-granted social structures. Many organizational endeavors are more dependent on the sharing of understandings (reliability) than on their correctness (validity).

Shared understandings are the basis for conversations among human actors, conversations that lead the actors to imagine a common experience, permit them to coordinate their actions more easily, and help them to shape and enforce social norms of justice (Bartel and Garud 2009). In the language of classical organization theory, stories and models are devices by which uncertainty is absorbed (March and Simon 1958, 164–66). They allow action to take place within comprehensible stories rather than incomprehensible reality. Convergence on a story of group history is particularly important. In that spirit, Benedict Anderson (1991) argued that a sense of nationality involves understandings of an imagined community built on a constructed history through a judicious combination of amnesia, invention, and interpretation.

Such understandings are also significant factors in creating a viable social system of justice. Justice is a difficult aspiration to define and to achieve. It requires broad agreement within a society on elements of fairness and on individual and social responsibilities. The stories and models of high-intellect learning are part of the apparatus by which such agreement is obtained. They facilitate social convergence of belief and individual and social confidence in intelligence.

At the same time, storytelling provides a basis for social approval. Being able to tell a sharable and interesting story of experience is an important aspect of the intelligence both of participants and of scholars. The ability to tell a convincing, high-intellect story about experience marks a superior manager, a superior researcher, and a superior consultant. Developing such capabilities is a primary responsibility of organizations. In that spirit, John Stuart Mill wrote, "The first element of good government being the virtue and intelligence of the human beings composing the community, the most important point of excellence which any form of government can possess is to promote the virtue and intelligence of the people themselves" ([1861] 1962, 32). Thus, life in organizations is marked by a quest for stories and models of maximum comprehensible complexity, an interpretation of life that is simultaneously suitably interesting and suitably comprehensible to signal intelligence, and for the development of individuals who can expound such interpretations.

Beauty

The Anglican struggle over retaining the King James translation of the Bible in spite of its translation confusions, or the more general struggle within Jewish, Muslim, and Christian communities over challenges to the historical accuracy of biblical accounts, are reminders that beauty and veracity are not necessarily codeterminate. Keats's proposition that "beauty is truth, truth beauty" is an enchanting idea but not readily demonstrable. In the prosaic domains of ordinary life, it seems obvious that many things that are true about human existence are far from beautiful, and many things that are beautiful are not true.

Beauty, truth, and justice are independent components of virtue, but beauty is not a lesser value than the others. The classic trinity of scholarly worth does not subordinate one value to any of the others (Lave and March 1975). Nowhere is that independent autonomy more important than in stories of organizations. Organizational life is given value by the ability to tell a story of beauty about it. Ideas are a form of art (March 2008, chap. 1).

It is a vision that resonates with the better examples of the organization storytelling craft. When John Padgett and his colleagues describe the origins of Florentine political and economic organization (Padgett and Ansell 1993; Padgett and McLean 2006), or Karl Weick (1996) describes the reaction of a firefighting crew to crisis, or Steven Barley (1986) describes the way in which CAT technicians make sense of their machines, or Charles Perrow (1984) describes the orchestration of accidents, the stories are beautiful. When Harrison White (1970) describes vacancy chains, or Albert Hirschman (1970) describes the trade-offs among exit, voice, and loyalty, or Thomas Schelling (1978) derives macro implications from micro motives, or William Feller (1968) describes stochastic processes, the models are beautiful. The beauty is neither incidental nor guaranteed. It is carefully crafted and not reliably exhibited in the stories and models produced by others.

Even a casual reading of the history of human civilizations suggests that the production and appreciation of objects that provide aesthetic pleasure are significant aspirations of intelligence. Nietzsche described the historian's job as "inventing ingenious variations on a probably commonplace theme, in raising the popular melody to a universal symbol and showing what a world of depth, power and beauty exists in it" (1957, 37–38). It is not a bad job description for those who would capture the lessons of experience through stories and models.

4
GENERATING NOVELTY

Although there are numerous unresolved problems, theories of adaptation deal reasonably well with the efficiencies and surprises associated with the processes by which existing ideas, practices, forms, or products survive and reproduce (Cyert and March 1963; March 1988, chap. 8; 1994; 1999a, chap. 15; Nelson and Winter 1982; Hannan and Freeman 1989; Cohen and Sproull 1996; March, Schulz, and Zhou 2000; Hodgkinson and Starbuck 2008). Theories of adaptation typically deal less well with the exploratory processes by which new ideas, forms, products, or practices are created, made available, and protected from premature elimination (Becker, Knudsen, and March 2006). These latter processes and notions about them constitute the rudiments of a theory of novelty and are the focus of this chapter.

Two preliminary caveats may be worth recording. The first is that a theory of novelty deals primarily with *global* novelty, not *local* novelty. It focuses on the generation of attributes or practices that are new to a population of organizations, not just new to the organization to which they spread. Theories of the spread of things are essential to understanding organizational innovation and adaptation, but they are somewhat different from theories of the generation of new ideas. In particular, a primary feature of local innovativeness is the base level of ignorance in the innovator. To a novice lover, all techniques of lovemaking are exciting discoveries, regardless of their familiarity to others. Likewise, an experienced scholar is less inclined to claim originality than is a beginner.

The second caveat is that studies of novelty and creativity are sometimes confused by a tendency to conflate the two. Novelty is deviation from established procedures or knowledge; creativity is novelty that is subsequently judged successful. Novelty is a necessary, but not sufficient, condition for creativity. Thus, many of the individual and social attributes that lead to novelty will also lead to creativity, but the complications of identifying the social and competitive processes by which novelty is confirmed as creativity are ignored by a theory of novelty.

In addition, this chapter treats two assumptions as more or less self-evident. The first is that most novel ideas are bad ones—that is, they will subsequently be judged unsuccessful. Only a small, unpredictable fraction of novel initiatives will turn out to be successful. The second assumption is that when novel ideas are generated, there is no reliable way to anticipate which of them will be successful. The few novel ideas that will prove to be creative are indistinguishable from those that will not until considerable time has passed. These two properties of novelty are critical to understanding the problems with novelty.

ADAPTATION AS AN ENEMY OF NOVELTY

The proposition that humans conserve beliefs and practices and thus are hostile to novelty is well known to the study of social psychology (Lord, Ross, and Lepper 1979; Nickerson 1998). It is also characteristic of learning from experience. As we observed in chapter 2, new rules, routines, forms, and ideas are disadvantaged by the way the replication of success leads to increasing stability in choice. This is partly because novel things have properties that place them at risk. Their outcome distributions tend to have low means and high variances; they often require practice; their returns are often delayed in time and are often global rather than local. It is also partly because the replication of success tends to find a satisfactory (possibly because of chance) alternative and stick with it, particularly if alternatives require practice in order to realize their potential. The replication of success reduces the likelihood of throwing good money after bad, but it also means that good alternatives with poor initial results will be permanently passed over.

Similarly, as pointed out in chapter 3, learning through the construction of stories and models is implicitly hostile to novelty. Stories and models are created out of familiar elements linked together in familiar ways. The familiarity and flexibility of story and model frames make them endure and thereby provide a barrier to new experience or new frames. New things are not experienced because they are coded into narratives and models that preserve existing frames and thereby, in an important sense, do not occur as episodes from which new lessons can be learned. The proposition that there is nothing new under the sun is a proposition as much about the stories that are told and the models that are created as it is about the reality they purport to understand. The construction of stories and models of experience out of familiar themes assures that the lessons of experience will be easily understood and readily assimilated, but it also inhibits new themes and new interpretations. The novelty that will endure is primarily novelty that can be assimilated into old stories and models, which tends to exclude extremely deviant items (March 1992).

Because of these features of adaptation to experience, one of the more common themes of research on adaptation and of the literatures on technological, organizational, or intellectual change is the notion that novelty is not favored by adaptive processes (Garud, Nayyar, and Shapira 1997; Van de Ven 1999). New, deviant ideas are likely to be bad ones (Simonton 1995, 1999; Sutton 2002), and any general inclination to invent and reproduce new ideas is likely to lead to disaster. Moreover, even good new ideas are likely to lead to unfavorable results in the near temporal and spatial distance and thus are unlikely to endure long enough to exhibit their potential value.

Processes that produce actions having a large number of

negative outcomes and only a small number of positive ones, most of which are delayed considerably or realized at a distance from the locus of adaptation, are prime candidates for elimination by adaptive processes, even though their expected value may qualify them for survival (Denrell and March 2001; Denrell 2007). In part, this is because adaptive processes, as we normally observe and model them, are myopic. They are relatively insensitive to outcomes that are separated in time or space from the locus of adaptation (Levinthal and March 1993; Levinthal and Posen 2008). This feature of adaptation underlies problems of delayed gratification (self-control) and distant gratification (altruism). It also underlies problems with novelty.

The tendency toward eliminating variability is strengthened by diffusion from others. An important mechanism for the replication of successful practices, routines, and forms is the spread of rules through a connected population (Strang and Soule 1998). Imitation leads to homogenization of practices across individuals and organizations that are connected in such a way that their attributes are visible (DiMaggio and Powell 1983; Djelic 1998). Diffusion of practices among connected organizations is limited by well-known difficulties of reproducing routines (Czarniawska and Sevón 1996, 2005), but it results in considerable convergence and the reduction of variation, particularly where the likelihood of imitating an attribute is increased by the number of organizations exhibiting the attribute (Singh, Tucker, and House 1986; Carroll and Hannan 1989; Hannan 1998).

In short, exploitation drives out exploration (March and

Simon 1958, 185; Holland 1975; March 1999c, chap. 7). It seems likely that a theory of novelty will have to provide an understanding of how processes that generate novelty and heterogeneity can survive in the face of processes of refinement and imitation that seem likely to eliminate novelty and its progenitors if they themselves are to survive (Van de Ven 1999; Nooteboom 2000).

THE NOVELTY PUZZLE

Novelty is vulnerable to adaptive processes. Yet new ideas and changes stemming from them, as well as heterogeneity in routines, practices, and forms, are conspicuous aspects of modern organizational experience. Although students of organizations often portray organizations as resistant to novelty and prone to mimetic homogeneity, a comparison of almost any organization as it functions today with the same organization fifty years ago reveals substantial differences, and contemporaneous heterogeneity among organizations is often considerable (Hoopes and Madsen 2008). Organizations are often difficult to change in any particular desired direction, and the complaints of organizational reformers pursuing a specific reform are, therefore, undoubtedly justified. However, organizational change is frequent (March 1999c, chap. 8), and proposals of organizational change are even more frequent. The babble of proposed change is loud and continuous.

Although not all change involves the introduction of novel

ideas, novelty is remarkably common. Deviant behaviors and practices are generated at a significant rate more or less continually. Most novel ideas are quickly and beneficially extinguished, but for some reason, this does not seem to slow the flow of novelty. The ultimate destiny of an evolving human species in an evolving universe may, in some sense, be a novelty-free existence, but adaptive processes seem likely to eliminate the species long before they eliminate novelty. Novelty appears in many respects to be irrepressible.

The failure of adaptive processes to eliminate foolishness, curiosity, deviance, and the processes of novelty is a puzzle. How do the mechanisms of novelty generation—whatever they may be—survive and reproduce (Dosi 1988; Dosi, Marengo, Bassanini, and Valente 1999; Gigerenzer 2000; Olsen 2009)? If most novel practices, products, or ideas diminish the chances of success—as seems almost axiomatic—what sustains mechanisms of novelty?

One might imagine that mechanisms of novelty survive despite their poor short-run and nearby returns by virtue of their more distant adaptive usefulness. One version of such an imagination is the speculation that the human organism is hardwired to foster novelty through a curiosity drive or other similar attribute that has evolved over thousands of generations. Such a speculation is, however, more a proclamation of faith than a certifiable phenomenon, and students of adaptive processes are generally reluctant to assume adaptive magic without understanding the specific way in which it has been accomplished.

It is possible to specify situations in which attributes that are locally suboptimal but more useful in the long run or over a broader perspective survive over time; but it is also possible to specify environments in which attributes essential to long-run survival, such as novelty or diversity, make survival in the short run difficult or impossible, and attributes that permit short-run survival are deleterious in the long run. There is no necessary solution to the problem of meeting both nearby and more distant survival requirements, and the precise mechanisms involved have to be identified.

The problem is complicated by the undoubted role of exploitative knowledge in the development and execution of novel ideas. Many studies of creativity identify the creative tension between processes of imagination and processes of execution, recognizing the extent to which the foolishness of exploration has to be juxtaposed to the discipline of exploitation. Either alone is not enough. It is usually argued, however, that the relation has to evolve in such a way that the ratio of imagination to the discipline of conventional knowledge is high relatively early in any particular project and declines over time. The usual concern is that the ratio tends to decline more rapidly than is desirable and thus that novel ideas are normalized too quickly.

TWO THEORETICAL TRACKS FOR UNDERSTANDING NOVELTY

Novelty is a conspicuous feature of organization life, so any simple idea that the adaptive efficiencies coded into knowledge and adaptive processes are homogeneously inimical to the generation of novelty or the reproduction of novelty-generating mechanisms is probably incomplete. In attempting to understand the survival of novelty in the face of adaptive mechanisms that seem likely to extinguish it, students of adaptation have developed theories of novelty along two main tracks, each of which offers insight but neither of which has led to a strikingly satisfactory resolution.

Adaptive Combinations

The first track postulates some kind of process by which new elements are produced from combinations of established old ones. The classic example in evolutionary biology is sexual reproduction and the genetic combinations that it produces. The classic example in organizational studies is the transfer of rules, routines, or practices from one location to another and the transformations that they experience as they combine with existing rules, routines, and practices within the receiving organization (Czarniawska and Sevón 1996, 2005; Zbaracki 1998). The search for a theory of the combinatorics of organizational routines has occupied many good people for many years. Progenitors of the ideas are found in economics (Schumpeter 1934), psychology (Hebb 1949), and political science (Deutsch 1963).

The combinatoric tradition has numerous contemporary contributors (Padgett and Ansell 1983; Feldman 1989, 2000; Pentland and Rueter 1994; Romer 1994; Pentland 1995; Cohen and Sproull 1996; Czarniawska and Joerges 1996;

Weitzman 1998; Gilboa and Schmeidler 2001; Feldman and Pentland 2003; Nooteboom 2000; Padgett, Lee, and Collier 2003; Gavetti, Levinthal, and Rivkin 2005; Obstfeld 2005; Padgett and McLean 2006; Becker, Knudsen, and March 2006; Gavetti and Warglien 2007; Page 2007; Svejenova, Mazza, and Planellas 2007; Nooteboom and Stam 2008).

The hunt for analogues has wandered from Mendel to linguistics to literary theory to haute cuisine to chemistry to neural networks with inconclusive but instructive results. The classic problems, particularly in theories of organizational novelty, are specifying precisely the basic elements involved, the laws of combination, and the ways in which those laws have evolved. Although elements of such a theory have been sketched in interesting ways, none of these problems has been solved in a way that is totally satisfactory. Nothing analogous to Mendelian laws exists for the theory of combinatoric novelty in organizations.

Adaptive Inefficiency

The second track of theories of novelty proceeds from the implicit assumption that processes of adaptation eliminate sources of error but are inefficient in doing so. Casual observations of human life suggest that existing mechanisms of adaptation are far from perfect. The modern social order is an impressively effective system of social control, but it is persistently subject to the contradictions of deviant actors, not all of whom spend years in prisons or asylums. Markets, particularly financial markets, enforce many elements of efficient adaptation, but they leave ample room for wonder at their inefficiencies. Successful gambling casinos and lotteries are monuments to human capabilities to make investment choices that reduce their prospects for wealth accumulation.

The propensity of managers in organizations to be similarly inattentive both to what is known and to evidence about what might come to be known is legendary (Pfeffer and Sutton 2006; Gary, Dosi, and Lovallo 2008), as is the failure of organizations to adopt practices reputed to have led to successes elsewhere. A common interpretation of such elements of apparent maladaptation emphasizes the relatively slow character of adaptive processes relative to the rate of change of the environments they encounter, but such an explanation suffers from the flexibility in estimating the rates of change that it allows.

At least at first blush, it appears that novelty survives not because it offers selective advantage within specifiable adaptive mechanisms but because those mechanisms are actually quite inefficient instruments of improvement and thus inefficient in eliminating the instruments of novelty. They move slowly, and they make mistakes. They have difficulty achieving unity and coherence. As a result, organizations exhibit a rich mixture of continuity and change (Olsen 2009). For example, in an organizational setting, personnel retention procedures that retain apparently successful managers and dismiss apparently unsuccessful managers seem prima facie to be useful in improving the fit of an organization to its environment; yet they can systematically retain less competent managers and dismiss the more competent, thus both tolerating foolish novelty and reducing the long-run fit (March and March 1977; Levinthal 1991; Denrell and Fang 2007).

Generic Labels

One conventional approach to talking about adaptive inefficiency is to provide a generic label for inexplicable deviations: stupidity? madness? revelation? genius? perversity? irreducible noise? The obvious analogue is the concept of mutation, a label for inexplicable deviations in genetic reproduction. Providing such labels is not an entirely foolish solution. Most natural processes or understandings of them exhibit inexplicable variation, and almost every domain of knowledge has labels for its unexplained variance: personality, power, leadership, culture. Since in social science generally, as in theories of adaptation, the unexplained variance is large, the concepts specified by such labels account for a great deal without explaining it (Lave and March 1975).

Such labeling is a kind of intellectual last resort that can be justified primarily by the extent to which it stimulates scholarship that reduces the use of the label. For example, some years ago, the label of "risk preference" was introduced into choice theory as a generic label for observed nonlinearities in the revealed human utility for money over alternative gambles and thus for unexplained deviations from predicted behavior. This led to considerable effort to unpack the nonlinearities, an effort that has sometimes been confused by the label but that has, on balance, probably been fruitful (March and Shapira 1987, 1992; March 1999c, chap. 15; Denrell 2007, 2008).

THE SURVIVAL OF MECHANISMS OF NOVELTY

An alternative to providing a catchall label for instances of novelty is to try to identify specific processes that generate unavoidable but predictable mistakes of adaptation. For example, we can imagine a theory of knowledge decay. Knowledge can be assumed to be accumulated through adaptation and stored in libraries, genes, rules, and memories. Knowledge is lost through turnover, forgetting, and misfiling, which assure that at any point there is considerable ignorance. Something that was once known is no longer known. In addition, knowledge is lost through its incomplete accessibility. Something that is known at one place is unknown at another (Jeppesen and Lakhani 2009).

Ignorance, whether from lags in adaptation, from decay, or from failure to access distributed knowledge, ordinarily is more likely to produce disaster than useful discovery; but sometimes it can generate the latter (Polanyi 1963). It is one of the reasons to be cautious in seeking to produce fully integrated, efficient systems of knowledge (Burt 1987). Better-articulated theories both of knowledge decay and of the peculiarities of access to distributed knowledge would almost certainly contribute to a better understanding of organizational novelty.

Novelty as Deviance

A conspicuous feature of novelty is that it deviates from received knowledge or norms, and a more general theory of deviance from conventionality might, therefore, illuminate a theory of novelty (Amabile 1983; Wells et al. 2006). One variant of a theory of deviance highlights the speculation that the deviants of creativity may share important attributes with the deviants from sanity and social norms. By this presumption, the correlates of genius will overlap considerably the correlates of delinquency. As a result, insofar as it focuses on individual-level explanations, a theory of novelty is likely to share many features with a theory of deviance. It is tempting to assume that creativity (i.e., novelty that turns out to change things) is simply a random draw from the universe of foolishness and thus that the primary nonrandom determinants of individual creativity are the determinants of deviance.

At least since Durkheim (1973), sociological theories of deviance have emphasized the way in which deviance is generated not by individual-level processes but by features of society. The strong association of criminal deviation with gender, race, and age attributes of individuals is pictured as stemming from properties of social structure: deviance stems from disassociation from well-integrated social institutions and norms. Alienation or separation from social institutions is created and sustained by the development of cultures of opposition and membership in deviant social groups (Becker 1963; Spergel 1964), by cultural typing (Said 1978), and by learning (Bandura 1977). Just as the innovative deviance of the juvenile delinquent (Becker 1984) is shaped by an imperfect relation with social institutions, norms, and instruments of control, so also perhaps is the innovative deviance of the entrepreneurial capitalist.

In order for a theory of deviance to contribute to a theory of novelty, however, it needs to explain how deviance fits into an adaptive system, how the inefficiencies of adaptation are inherent in its capabilities for producing successes. This is one way of perceiving the combinatorics of sexual reproduction among animals, or the combinatorics of the spread of ideas through a population of firms. Sexual reproduction generally produces combinations of genes that will be favored by the environment, but it also sometimes produces combinations that are exceptionally deviant. Most of these will fail miserably, but some small fraction will turn out to have attributes that are unusually favorable.

In an analogous fashion, the imitation of successful practices generally results in improved chances of survival, but it also can result in transformations that are exceptionally deviant. Again, most of these will fail miserably, but some small fraction will turn out to have attributes that are unusually favorable (Zbaracki 1998; Czarniawska and Sevón 2005). Similar things can be said about random interdisciplinary or cross-cultural interaction (March 2008, chap. 13). By embedding them in processes of efficient reproduction of favorable traits, selective adaptation preserves mechanisms for producing foolish novelty.

Adaptive Generation of Conditions for Novelty in Organizations

Three ways in which effective adaptation in organizations creates conditions favorable to novelty generation, even though the return from such novelty may be negative, are well known in organizational studies (for a further discussion, see Miner, Haunschild, and Schwab 2003). The first is the way in which success leads to *organizational slack* and its associated reduction in control, which in turn yields experimentation and avoidance of the infant mortality of ideas (Cyert and March 1963; Nohria and Gulati 1996; Greve 2003). Among start-up firms, excess capital resources provide slack buffers that limit the infant mortality of novel ideas (Levinthal 1991). In effect, substantial success, either in performance or in soliciting early support, absorbs the negative effects of failure and reduces the close monitoring of idea initiatives. These slack buffers reflect uncommitted resources (Deutsch 1963) that facilitate the extended pursuit of untested ideas, some small fraction of which may turn out to be exceptionally good ones (Winter 1971). Slack is produced by efficiency, but it serves to protect foolishness from elimination. Novelty (which is likely to be mostly foolish) is a side consequence of slack, which is a side consequence of effective adaptation.

A second phenomenon of organizational adaptation that

contributes to novelty is *managerial hubris.* Adaptive mechanisms retain successful managers at a higher rate than unsuccessful ones. A history of success leads managers to a systematic overestimation of the prospects for success in novel endeavors. If managers attribute their successes to talent when they are, in fact, a joint consequence of talent and good fortune, successful managers will come to believe that they have capabilities for beating the odds in the future as they apparently have had in the past. This hubris on the part of managers will lead them (and thereby their organizations) to be more supportive of novel risky ideas than the ideas warrant (March and Shapira 1987; Kahneman and Lovallo 1993). Novelty is a side consequence of managerial hubris about risk, which is a side consequence of adaptive managerial selection.

A third organizational feature contributing to novelty comes from the way competition among alternatives within or among organizations leads to overly *optimistic hopes* for novel ideas. In a competitive world of promises, winning projects are systematically projects in which hopes exceed reality (Wilson 1977; Harrison and March 1984; Thaler 1988). Novel ideas, by virtue of the lack of reliable knowledge about them, profit particularly from this tendency toward overoptimism. Competitive selection based on expectations for the future favors optimistic biases, which favor novelty because the uncertainty surrounding new things makes them more open to the enthusiasms of optimistic fantasy. A key U.S. government official involved in funding spy satellite systems noted that sixteen of the eighteen government space programs opened to competitive bidding between 1977 and 2002 were awarded to new players. He explained this as stemming from some combination of naiveté and guile: "You as the incumbent are probably going to write a realistic proposal because you know what's involved and propose pretty much what you've been doing, since it has been successful. Your competitor, out of ignorance or guile, is going to write a more imaginative, creative proposal for which there is almost no backing" (Taubman 2007).

The mechanisms underlying organizational slack, managerial hubris, and competitive optimism are all instruments of adaptive effectiveness. They reflect and support success, but at the same time they contribute to novelty in organizations even though novelty is, on average, a bad idea. These apparent paradoxes lead to the speculation that there may be other ways in which adaptive processes help to sustain, rather than eliminate, novelty-generating mechanisms.

Consider, for example, the ways in which intelligence and knowledge are implicated in the reproductive errors of adaptation (March 2008, chap. 8). On the one hand, intelligence and knowledge generally seem more likely to eliminate novelty than to sustain it. Substantially novel ideas, routines, and properties are likely to deviate from established practices and knowledge. They will generally be identified as inferior to existing practice by conventional intelligence. In the overwhelming majority of cases, rejection of new ideas by the application of intelligence proves to be sensible. The result is the reinforcement of the use of intelligence and knowledge in taking action, as well as in assessing novel practices. Predilections for using knowledge and intelligence are learned from good experience with them. Since they (correctly) identify most novel ideas as inferior, knowledge and intelligence are often portrayed both as major engines of competitive advantage, change, and economic growth (Winter 1987; Hatchuel and Weil 1995; Loasby, 1999) and as major inhibitors of creativity (Simonton 1999; March 2008, chap. 8).

However, there is another side to intelligence, what might be called utopian intelligence. Enthusiasm for rational intelligence leads to enthusiasm for ideas generated from abstract thinking and models, stimulates faith in the fit of hypothetical models to real situations, and encourages confidence in novel alternatives generated by abstract thinking. This kind of utopian intelligence appears to be a major source of novel ideas and to have produced well-documented cases of significant change. As might be expected, however, most such novel inventions end in disaster, as they have generally in the history of utopian idealists. Consider, for example, the role of utopian intelligence in the central planning of the Soviet Union and its Eastern European satellites, the American adventure in Vietnam, and the burst bubble of Long-Term Capital Management.

With such a record of disasters, even the crudest kind of adaptive process might be expected to extinguish the use of utopian intelligence. How does it happen, then, that utopian intelligence is reproduced in human communities? A possible answer (borrowed from population biology) is the idea of *hitchhiking* (Hedrick 1982). A property that is neutral or harmful survives by virtue of its linkage to a selectively advantageous property. An attribute (utopian intelligence) that almost always fails hitchhikes on an attribute (routine intelligence) that is frequently and manifestly successful.

The notion that mechanisms of novelty generation survive by hitchhiking on mechanisms of routine efficiency has appeal as an interpretation of one way in which an adaptive process might sustain novelty, but it leaves the conditions for hitchhiking unexplained. What links utopian intelligence with routine intelligence so that the hitchhiking occurs? The obvious (but not particularly helpful) answer is that the two elements of intelligence are linked cognitively and socially to such a degree that they cannot easily be unbundled. They share so many basic elements that an adaptive advantage of one necessarily results in an adaptive advantage for the other. For example, the two elements of intelligence are deeply intertwined in education so that success using one is highly correlated with success using another.

Hitchhiking as used in such an explication, however, is little more than an arm-wave reminder of adaptive inefficiencies. The intuitive idea is that mechanisms of adaptation create a dynamic of novelty that, despite its propensity to disaster, is shielded from elimination by the adaptive process itself. Developing that intuitive idea into something more precise requires a close empirical look at cases of novelty generation from the point of view of understanding how they survive their errors. The hitchhiking relation between routine intelligence and utopian intelligence provides a minimal specification of the mechanism, but it is only slightly less mysterious than the intuitive idea itself.

What other linkages exist that bundle organizational attributes so that it is difficult to separate their adaptive fates? An obvious feature of historical causality is its complexity. As the causal complexity of the bundling of organizational attributes increases, the amount of adaptive experience required to guarantee that adaptive processes will reliably reproduce only superior attributes becomes much larger than organizational experience can be expected to be. Under such conditions, novelty becomes not so much an anomaly of adaptation as a product of it, and a theory of novelty becomes a theory of the mechanisms of inherent adaptive inefficiency.

The problem is to move from a general proposition that the causal complexity of history sustains instruments of adaptive inefficiency from which elements of novelty arise to a more precise specification of individual mechanisms. Such a move will probably require two interrelated things. The first is empirical—an intense multiobservation focus over some time, a strategy that is probably more akin to the story of Mendelian research than to the story of Schumpeterian imagination. The second is theoretical—the development of a handful of precise ideas that clarify the phenomena that have been observed. Neither can proceed very far without the other, but it is particularly difficult to choose among quite different theoretical analogues without a precise linkage with empirical observations. For example, an argument that organizational development is akin to language development is prima facie reasonable, but it cannot really be assessed relative to arguments that organizational development is analogous to species development or chemical bonding without both precise specifications and careful comparisons of the alternatives with multiple empirical cases.

THE ENGINEERING OF NOVELTY

Organizational and social engineers seek ideas about possible organization forms or governmental procedures that might affect the rate of novelty or the success rate of novelty (Nooteboom and Stam 2008). One obvious possibility that has attracted considerable effort is to find early ways to distinguish the rare novel idea that will prove very successful from the numerous novel ideas that will be unsuccessful, even disastrous. The evidence does not support great optimism on this score, particularly with respect to extremely deviant ideas. New ideas that subsequently have changed knowledge considerably have usually been disparaged initially (Aronson 1977; David 1991). Strategies for distinguishing creativity from foolishness ordinarily impose criteria of conventionality that are more likely to reduce novelty than to purify it usefully. As Marc Andreessen, one of the founders of Netscape, said in an interview (Levy 2003), "Fundamental change comes out of left field. It has to be an idea that's viewed as crazy at the time. If any idea looks like a good idea, there are lots of big companies out there like Microsoft that would already be doing it" (E10).

A more promising alternative is to seek ways to minimize the costs of experimenting with new ideas while retaining the benefits of successful ones (Romano 2002; Holahan, Weil, and Wiener 2003). Organizational engineering seeks forms of organizational foolishness that are protected enough to generate modest amounts of novelty without being so favored as to swamp an organization with novel, but inferior, possibilities. However, devising structures or procedures that protect an organization from the costs of deviance without also inhibiting the recognition and implementation of the occasional good idea is not easy (Cohen and Levinthal 1989, 1990). A classic solution is to limit the "bet size" of investments in novelty. The idea is to differentiate among novel ideas by small-scale experiments and to recoup the costs (including the losses associated with bad ideas) by subsequently increasing the investments in successful projects (Brown and Eisenhardt 1995; McGrath 1999).

The strategy of limiting exploratory bet size has achieved a certain amount of popularity (Sitkin 1992; Bowman and Hurry 1993); it has also generated a certain amount of skepticism (Adner and Levinthal 2004). There are obvious difficulties involved in scaling up from small experiments to large programs, but where that is possible, the strategy seems potentially feasible. It is, for example, one view of the plethora of entrepreneurial start-ups found during the heyday of Silicon Valley experimentation. Not by intentional design but primarily by happenstance, the high-tech community stumbled on a financial structure that, at least in the short run, seemed to separate the impact of the costs of experimentation from the realization of its benefits and allowed investors in the occasional spectacular success to bear the fruits of that success without fully paying the costs of the large number of failures.

Another set of strategies involves partitioning an organization into diverse subgroups. For example, a standard idea in discussions of combinatorics as a source of novelty is the advantage of diversity in routines for producing instances of advantageous novelty through high-variance combinations of them (Mayr 1982; Potvin, Kraenzel, and Seutin 2001; Page 2007). Diversity in organizations tends to be reduced by the homogenizing tendencies of adaptation (Beecher-Monas 2007), but it is maintained by boundaries that create what Nooteboom (2000) describes as "secluded niches." Permeable boundaries and the parochialism they stimulate encourage homogenization within their limits but diversity across them. As a result, they can sustain both diversity and adequate contact to allow useful combinations (Krackhardt and Kilduff 1990; Oberoi 1994; March 2008, chap. 13).

The organizational problem is to maintain parochialism among subunits sufficient to sustain multiple disciplined knowledge systems but with cross-unit contact sufficient to share ideas and practices (Burt 1987; Galunic and Rodan 1998; Rodan and Galunic 2004; Fang, Lee, and Schilling, 2009). The optimum level of segregation is difficult to specify, involving as it does difficult trade-offs across space and time (March 1994, chap. 6). Any solution to this problem has to be sensitive to the technology and organization of contact, as is evidenced by contemporary discussions of the advantages and disadvantages of changing capabilities to access distributed knowledge (Powell, Koput, and Smith-Doerr 1996; Rodan 2008).

Early experiments in strengthening links among disparate knowledge bases have led to remarkable discoveries of ideas and practices that have developed in previously isolated domains (Jeppesen and Lakhani 2009). It seems possible, however, that a side consequence of improving knowledge diffusion might be to introduce elements of homogenization that limit the decentralized pursuit of unlikely ideas. The history of organizational cycling between centralization and decentralization is a tribute, in part, to the engineering difficulty of finding an enduring balance between the short-run and local costs and the long-run and more global benefits of boundaries.

5

THE LESSONS OF EXPERIENCE

Learning from experience in organizations is both an important phenomenon and a large industry. Business schools, publishers, publications, and consultants offer advice to business firms in parallel with an overlapping collection of schools, publishers, publications, and consultants specializing in public-sector organizations. To some extent, the groups flourish by equating improvement with learning, thus making the proposition that learning is a good thing into a tautology, but they provide ideas about how to achieve a "learning organization," by which they mean an organization that uses mechanisms of learning to improve the return from actions. Some of the ideas come from research, some from experience, some from analysis, and some from various forms of personal imagination. They all seek to provide clues to improving organizational adaptiveness.

The efforts reflect a widespread belief that organizations need to improve their capabilities for comprehending and adapting to their environments (Argyris and Schön 1978; Etheredge 1985; Olsen and Peters 1996). The strategies for doing so include exploiting the learning found in academic theories of management and organization as translated and advocated by the purveyors of organizational advice. They also include developing capabilities for reacting intelligently to the lessons of direct experience. In this tradition, failures to improve intelligence through experience are due to human faults that are correctable through education and training.

The previous chapters have provided a few footnotes to those beliefs and efforts. They have explored some selected aspects of the possibilities, ambiguities, and problems of learning from experience. At the risk of using a few words to communicate what more words have already said, four general conclusions might be suggested.

- First, organizations and the people in them seek intelligence by modifying their expectations and understandings on the basis of the actions they take and the outcomes they observe. They learn both through low-intellect mechanisms that simply replicate successful actions, routines, or forms and also through high-intellect mechanisms that develop theories, models, and stories of history. Modifications in behaviors and understandings on the basis of experience are conspicuous aspects of human existence.
- Second, these mechanisms lead to palpable improvements in domains of relatively constrained activities that are repeated frequently. In such situations, the experience gained from repetitive practice frequently improves performance,

although it ordinarily does not lead to an optimum, is subject to inadequate experimentation, and has limited generalizability.

- Third, in situations involving more complex causal relationships and fewer repetitions, experience is not a good teacher in the sense of reliably providing a clear basis for improvement in performance. However, in combination with the mythic themes provided by models and accepted story themes, the interpretation of experience develops conversational agreement, a sense of comprehension, a certification of the primacy of the human intellect, and (sometimes) a modicum of aesthetic achievement.
- Fourth, learning from experience requires experimentation for its long-run effectiveness but tends to extinguish it. Novelty is habitually vulnerable to effective learning. Nevertheless, novelty does arise in organizations and can, to a limited extent, be engineered.

EXPERIENCE AS A USEFUL TEACHER

There is no question that individuals and organizations regularly and routinely learn from experience in the sense of modifying behavior and understandings on the basis of experience. What is less self-evident is whether the lessons so readily learned from experience reliably improve performance or the likelihood of survival.

Experience is a significant source of intelligence in relatively isolated, narrow domains of frequently exercised specialized capabilities. Many common repetitive situations involve concrete specific knowledge. They provide relatively clear signals, relatively low levels of noise, and relatively large samples—adequate information for valid inference and palpable learning. Gardeners learn about the growth of plants, and although direct experiential knowledge about gardening is likely to be filled with superstition and half truths if it is not supplemented with knowledge gleaned from systematic experiments, experienced farmers typically know more than novice ones.

In a similar way, organizations learn how to operate successfully in specific contexts in which they find themselves. That knowledge is likely to be limited in application and generality, but it represents the useful fruits of trial-and-error learning, imitation, and selection in narrow domains. In almost every kind of specialized human activity, experience effects are positive. Experience, however, is not a perfect teacher. The replication of success often results in improvement, but it is not a particularly good way of discovering the best among many alternatives.

Perhaps the best-known pieces of evidence for the value of experiential learning are found in studies of so-called learning curves (Argote and Epple 1990; Argote 1999; Argote and Todorova 2007). In a number of well-documented studies, the unit costs of producing products have been shown to decline at a decreasing rate with the cumulative number of units produced (i.e., with experience). The more widgets a factory has produced in the past, the lower the cost of producing the next widget. A classic example is the way increases in cumulative experience reduce the hours required to assemble an aircraft. Likewise, both the time required to complete surgical procedures and the number of complications from surgery have been found to decrease at a decreasing rate with experience (Pisano, Bohmer, and Edmondson 2001; Reagans, Argote, and Brooks 2005).

The rate of improvement varies substantially from one product/procedure or organization to another. Organizations also sometimes independently exhibit improvement at a decreasing rate with the passage of time, but those gains (perhaps attributable to technological improvement in the environment) are usually smaller. Although it is generally easier to observe experiential improvement in unit costs or productivity than it is to anticipate the parameters involved in advance or to specify observable adaptive processes that have clearly produced the results, unit costs decline with cumulative units produced across a relatively large number of production operations.

In a similar, but less documented, way, continuing relationships (e.g., partners, bosses/subordinates, vendors, competitors) and the development of technical or artistic skills involve repeated experiences in constrained settings that are marked by fairly reliable improvement over time. Signals are clear; noise levels are low; sample sizes of experience are substantial. Partners develop reputations that are relatively reliable. Practice usually improves technical performance; the capabilities of lovers, artists, and plumbers can normally be expected to increase with experience. Ignace Paderewski, the great pianist (and briefly in 1919 the prime minister of

Poland and signatory to the Treaty of Versailles), is reputed to have replied to praise from Queen Victoria that described him as a genius by saying "Perhaps, but before that I was a drudge."

EXPERIENCE AS AN IMPERFECT TEACHER

Despite its pervasiveness and the record of its successes, learning from experience faces numerous complications that limit its effectiveness. Underlying many of these complications are three conspicuous features of experience. The first is the vividness of experience; the second is the ambiguity of the lessons of experience; the third is the flexibility of interpretation.

Vividness of Experience

Direct experience is exceptionally vivid to the individual or organization experiencing it (Fischhoff 1975). The vividness of direct experience leads learners to exaggerate the information content of personal experience relative to other information. There are good reasons why any particular organization or individual might weight direct experience somewhat more heavily than the experience of others. For example, direct experience requires no generalization to demonstrate its relevance to the organization or person to whom it has occurred. However, the salience and dramatic force of experience combine with its difficulty of interpretation to make attempting to learn from experience a significant source of error. As Mark Twain observed, a cat that jumps on a hot stove is likely never to jump on any stove (hot or cold) again. As a result, the cat is likely to fail to discover the pleasures of jumping on cold stoves.

Consciousness of the problem does not reliably lead to doubts about experiential learning. The good sense of limiting attention to direct experience is overcome by the emotional force of the apparent lessons to be gained from experience. Consider, for example, a surgeon forming estimates of the risks of a surgical procedure. He or she has available extensive studies of the mortality rates associated with particular procedures, as well as recollections from his or her own experience. Since the risks associated with a particular surgeon are to some extent idiosyncratic to that surgeon, reflecting among other things the surgeon's skill, it is sensible for any particular surgeon to weigh direct experience somewhat more heavily than the individual experiences of other individuals; but the vividness of personal experience ordinarily results in its being weighted too heavily compared with the aggregate experiences of many individuals. Where the risks are extremely small, only a surgeon with considerable experience will accumulate a sample of procedures performed large enough to warrant any significant modification of the aggregate statistics. In particular, the skewed distribution of occurrences of a low-probability event assures that substantially more surgeons will have experiences better than the average than will have experiences worse than the average.

They will come to believe that the risks are less than they are.

Direct experience is similarly misleading in personnel decisions. Consider the frequent use of personal presentations or personal interviews in making hiring decisions. Such direct experiences are systematically more compelling than is warranted by the information they contain, and thus they typically are given too much weight. As a result, personal presentations, such as job talks, are more likely to degrade than to improve the effectiveness of personnel decisions. The erratic but compelling impressions of personal exposure overwhelm information gathered in a more systematic, more valid, but less compelling way (Dawes, Faust, and Meehl 1989).

Ambiguity of the Lessons of Experience

Experience has to be converted into lessons learned, and the conversion is both difficult and unending. As Simone de Beauvoir observed, "To declare that existence is absurd is to deny that it can ever be given a meaning; to say that it is ambiguous is to assert that its meaning is never fixed, that it must be constantly won" ([1948] 1980, 129). Knowing what happened is sometimes possible, though it is often difficult. Knowing why it happened, and thus being able to make inferences about the events of the past, involves forming implicit or explicit causal inferences in situations that invite debate and error.

The ambiguity of experience has many causes and takes

many forms, but a significant fraction of them can be summarized in terms of five attributes of experience:

- First, the causal structure of experience is *complex*. Many uncontrolled variables are involved, and their relations include multiple interactions and multiple colinearities. The relations among the variables may include numerous instances of feedback loops, a variety of time delays, and unknown functional forms. As a result, it is difficult to uncover the causal structure and to identify the effects of actions. For example, a legendary feature of organizational inference forming is the inclination to attribute outcomes (particularly favorable ones) to organizational actions in situations in which general economic or political conditions, the actions of others, and any number of other uncontrolled factors may contribute substantially. Moreover, many variables that seem likely to be important are difficult to observe and elusive to measure. As a result, the lessons derived from experiential learning are rife with unjustified conclusions, superstitious associations, misleading correlations, tautological generalizations, and systematic biases.
- Second, experience is *noisy.* The events of history are drawn from a distribution of possibilities, either because of errors in observation or interpretation or because the causal structure is truly stochastic. A particular realized history is likely to be a quite poor representation of the possibilities. As a result, learning from experience involves trying to learn not only from the actual events observed but also from the events that did not occur but might quite easily have oc-

curred. The generation of such hypothetical histories replaces evidence with imagination, with all the invitations to error that such a substitution involves.

• Third, history includes numerous examples of *endogeneity,* cases in which the properties of the world are affected by actions adapting to it. Capabilities are affected by practice, and the rate of practice is affected by the choices made. Organizations and their environments coevolve. The desires (wants) of actors affect actions, but the actions also affect the wants. History is a series of samples, but the sampling rates, and therefore the sampling errors, of the various alternatives are affected by the unfolding of experience.

• Fourth, history as it is known is *constructed* by participants and observers. Individuals learn not from history but from historical stories, including the stories they tell themselves, that are concocted for a purpose. The spin doctor was as familiar to the writing of Egyptian history or Norse sagas as he or she is today. Winston Churchill has been quoted as saying, "History will be kind to me, for I intend to write it." The proposition that the mean of lies converges to truth as the sample size increases is not easily demonstrated, either empirically or deductively.

• Fifth, history is *miserly* in providing experience. It offers only small samples and thus large sampling error in the inferences formed. If a statistician undertook to design an observational world that would frustrate inference, the resulting design might look a good deal like much of the natural experience of organizations. Organizations try to learn from small samples, often samples of one or fewer. They try to make inferences from observations of events involving unique, changing contexts and conditions. Without experimental control over key variables or a large sample of observations under varying (and observable) conditions, the search for causal identification is seriously compromised. Imagination becomes at least as significant as observation. As Marvin Minsky observed in contemplating the problems of artificial intelligence, "By themselves, simple learning systems are only useful in recurrent situations; they cannot cope with significant novelty. Nontrivial performance is obtained only when learning systems are supplemented with classification or pattern-recognition methods of some inductive ability. For the variety of objects encountered is so enormous that we cannot depend upon recurrence" (1963, 413).

The lessons of history can be hard to discern through participating in it. It is difficult for organizational participants to learn from experience, and their attempts to do so are prone to error (Mezias and Starbuck 2003; Baumard and Starbuck 2005). Experience often appears to increase significantly the confidence of successful managers in their capabilities without greatly expanding their understanding. The failures are not particularly due to weaknesses in managers or their training. Detecting the effects of variation in one or two factors in a complex system normally requires both holding other things constant and making big enough changes in the variables of interest to be detectable over the noise. In practice, organizations tend to change many things simultaneously and to make relatively small changes.

Flexible Interpretations

The events of ambiguous experience are given meaning through flexible interpretations. As the French poet-philosopher-historian Paul Valéry said, "History will justify anything. It teaches precisely nothing, for it contains everything and furnishes examples of everything" (quoted in White 1987, 36). Flexibility preserves mythic frames at the cost of weakening their predictive power. The trade-off makes more sense if the point is to preserve agreement on stories or to assure capabilities for explaining experience after the fact than it does if the point is to capture an extrastory reality or to use experience to predict the future. In general, stories and models are more commonly used for ex post explanations than for ex ante predictions.

Flexibility in interpretation is facilitated by natural language and symbolic abstractions and by the ways in which they are used. Natural language storytellers call forth meaning through language, particularly through metaphor (e.g., "learning," "exploration" and "exploitation," "decision," "power," "garbage can"). Mathematical storytellers similarly call forth meaning through abstract symbols that allow imaginative extensions—for example, the interpretation of models of the spread of disease as models of the spread of technology.

A flexible quest for shared understandings that seem intelligent is probably more served by the ambiguities of history than frustrated by them. Failures can be interpreted to preserve belief (Baumard and Starbuck 2005). If a revolution fails, it may be because it was a bad idea, but it also may be because it was not pursued with enough vigor. If a policy fails, the failure may be a consequence of the policy, but it also may be a consequence of social forces or of inadequate or malicious implementation. If a pilot experiences a near collision with another aircraft, it may be a warning of dangerous practice and treated as a failure, but it also may be taken as an indication of superior skill in avoiding a collision and treated as a success (Tamuz 1988).

Interpretive flexibility assures that any specific experience will be consistent with a variety of different lessons. For example, many stories build on evaluations, and many of the evaluations of the experiences of organizations or their managements are justified by observations that could as easily justify quite different evaluations (March 1994, 87–89). The same managerial behavior can be labeled as either "bold" or "impetuous," while its opposite can be labeled as either "careful" or "timid." The difference between an "arrogant" manager and a "self-assured" one can be as difficult to discern as the difference between an "insecure" manager and a "consultative" one. It is not that evaluative stories are indifferent to data. They typically draw upon them extensively. But just as the same face can easily produce quite different, even contradictory, portraits, the same observations of organizational experience can produce evaluations that differ profoundly.

There are other features of standard frames that facilitate fitting disparate experience into standard frames. For example, the stories and models of social science are filled with tautologies. Power is the capability to get what one wants; it is measured by the extent to which one gets what one wants. Individuals pursue their interests; their interests are inferred from what they pursue. Things that are not understood are given labels that provide a linguistic appearance of explanatory power but are better seen as admissions of a lack of understanding or as place markers for subsequent development. In the stories of psychology, "personality" often serves as a label for what is not understood—the unexplained variance. In the stories of sociology and anthropology, "culture" plays a similar role, as do "power" in political science, "utility" in economics, and "mutation" in evolutionary biology. In popular stories, "human nature" often serves a similar purpose. Such labels give stories an aura of stable verisimilitude while providing a flexible fit to experience. They typically provide great capabilities for creating stories of post hoc explanatory appeal but little or no predictive power or engineering leverage.

Avoiding the Problems of Experience

Perhaps because of the conspicuous problems in interpreting history, much of the knowledge used in organizations develops in ways somewhat different from those that might be expected from a conception of experience-based action. First, much of what is believed in organizations is a collection of derivations from simple assumptions. The entire apparatus of the economic theory of organizations, for example, has very little detailed empirical basis. It consists primarily in theorems derived from a few elementary propositions about human behavior. The great advantage of such an approach to knowledge is that one can demonstrate the correctness of the theorems as a technical matter rather than as a matter of inference from data. Derivations within theories of organizations include a number of verifiable, but not particularly startling, predictions, such as the idea that increasing the wages offered for a position will increase the number of people willing to take the job. They also contain a few instructive surprises, such as propositions about the "the tragedy of the commons," the "winner's curse," the "prisoners' dilemma," or "competency traps."

Second, much of what is believed about organizations derives from an engineering conception of knowledge. A full scientific conception of knowledge seeks to understand a system well enough to be able to anticipate the necessary subsequent condition of any possible antecedent conditions. An engineering conception of knowledge seeks a set of antecedent conditions sufficient to produce a particular subsequent condition. A child learning to ride a bicycle does not attempt to understand the full intricacies of bicycle dynamics but only a set of movements and responses adequate to sustain balance and movement. An organization looks for organizational forms, practices, and products that are adequate to achieve targets and to improve in a familiar situation. It does not seek to know the likely consequences of all possible combinations of forms, practices, and products under all conditions.

Third, rather than seeking to understand a complex world,

organizations often seek to create simpler worlds they can understand. Rather than build with materials freely available, they create materials with comprehensible and manageable attributes. Rather than try to understand the full richness of human behavior, they classify, train, and constrain human actors to make them comprehensible and manageable (Foucault 1961, 1975; Holmqvist 2008). Rather than depend on the future reliability of partners, they write contracts. Rather than run risks, they buy insurance. Rather than predict the outcomes of a gamble, they arbitrage among the differing expectations of others.

The Bottom Line

If there is one lesson to be gleaned from the explorations in this book, it is that learning from experience is an imperfect instrument for finding the truth. Much of organizational and managerial life will produce vividly compelling experiences from which individuals and organizations will learn with considerable confidence, but the lessons that they learn are likely to be incomplete, superstitious, self-confirming, or mythic. They will characteristically lead to suboptimal choices and are unlikely to yield valid characterizations of the causal processes underlying the experiences. Experience is likely to generate confidence more reliably than it generates competence and to stop experimentation too soon. As a result, there is a persistent disparity between the assurance with which advice is provided by experienced people and the quality of the advice. Berndt Brehmer (1980), the Swedish psychologist, summarized the evidence in a title for an article published in 1980: “In One Word: Not from Experience.” Experience may possibly be the best teacher, but it is not a particularly good teacher.

The observation is not that knowledge in general is impossible. Knowledge about human behavior can be impressive, but it is most impressive when it is embedded in stable cultural and institutional contexts or derived from settings where repeated, controlled observations are possible. In domains that are experienced less frequently and are less constrained, direct experience is often both less informative and more compelling. As a result, a subjective assurance of understanding derived from experience may be poorly correlated with genuine knowledge.

The contrast between the enthusiasms for experiential learning on the one hand and its deficiencies on the other have led to persistent efforts to discover alternative conceptions of inference more consistent with the possibilities of experience. Some of these procedures are effectively variations on multivariate statistics by which the underlying complexities are approximated through a combination of simple, generic models and large databases. They depend critically both on the efficacy of the simple models and on adequate numbers of observations. In ordinary experience, the former is doubtful and the latter is rare, so the usefulness of the technology is normally limited to large database formal research studies in domains in which the causal structure is transparent.

Alternatively, it is frequently argued that useful understanding of the causal basis of experience can be extracted from the small sample sizes of ordinary experience. Among others (e.g., Malan and Kriger 1998), I have argued that it is possible to learn from "samples of one or fewer" (March, Sproull, and Tamuz 1991). A similar argument runs through much of the advocacy of case studies (Herbst 1970; George and McKeown 1985; Mohr 1985), "thick description" (Geertz 1973; Gherardi 2006), and literature (Gagliardi and Czarniawska 2006; March 2008, chap. 18) as sources of knowledge.

The notion that it is possible to discern valid lessons about the world from detailed descriptions of specific episodes of ordinary experience finds an enthusiastic audience. It confirms the intuition and practice of most people. It reflects such a widely held belief that it is judicious to be cautious in denying it. However, it is hard to specify a theory of inference that sustains the idea unambiguously against a more conservative judgment of doubt. Although the literature exhibits a persistent aspiration that analyses based on rich descriptions and imagined histories may be linked to ideas about inference from empirical evidence, a conclusive justification of stories of experience as bases for genuine knowledge is more elusive than would be expected from the enthusiasm for it.

From the perspective of those who oppose it, the argument in favor of samples of one or fewer can be seen as an attempt to provide some kind of intellectual foundation for a deep human predilection to stories. Intellect is enlisted as an advocate for storytelling. Arguments are mobilized to provide a justification for the subjective sensations of pleasure and intelligence gained from converting instances of experience into possible understandings of the world. Since the ability and eagerness of human intellect to conjure utilitarian justifications for intuitive prejudices is one of the more endearing human traits, the efforts are often elegant and even persuasive.

Enthusiasm for learning from samples of one or fewer permeates ordinary life as well as much of social science and should not be summarily dismissed. In order to make the lessons from meager experience accessible, however, it is probably necessary to experience things richly, drawing on more aspects of history and more interpretations. It is probably necessary to consider events from the perspective of multiple preferences. It is probably necessary to supplement the data of history with the data of virtual experience, using "near histories" and hypothetical histories. In this way, the process of translating experience into understanding and understanding into action will often be an exercise of imagination that supplements or replaces data-based inference and logical derivation (March, Sproull, and Tamuz 1991).

EXPERIENCE AND HUMAN INTELLECT

The case for experiential knowledge as an effective instrument of adaptation is relatively weak in normal terms, but intelligence is not fully comprehended in terms of instrumental utility. In chapter 1, organizations were pictured as pursuing intelligence, and intelligence was presented as having two components. The first involves the instrumental utility of adaptation to the environment. The second involves the gratuitous interpretation of the nature of things through the use of human intellect. From the second point of view, experience is less a source of adaptive improvement than a stimulant to a fundamental human activity—the creation and decoration of irrelevant understanding.

Human intellect displays itself through curiosity about the world, through the gossip, conversations, stories, accounts, explanations, theories, and mythologies that (a) make existence meaningful in an interesting way (March and Sevón 1984), (b) provide rationalizations for willfulness (Feldman and March 1981), and (c) exhibit human imagination. Within such a perspective, understandings of experience are not so much instruments of life as they are life itself (Czarniawska 1997, 21); and the pursuit of meaning is less a method of effective adaptation than an essential activity of storytelling human beings (March and Olsen 1975, 1976; March 1994, 212–19).

Storytelling and the construction of models are elemental human activities by which human actors establish their own unique intelligence and the intellectuality of their species. In this perspective, storytelling and model building may be instrumental to adaptiveness, but that instrumentality is secondary to the differentiation that intellect provides, both among humans and among species. It is hard not to be charmed by such a vision of the intellectual primacy of irrelevant imagination. It strikes a chord that is sometimes drowned in the clatter of demands for utilitarian practicality. It conjures a dream of autonomy for intellect that glorifies one of the more distinct attributes of human existence. It grants an arbitrary status to the human mind. It is a kind of declaration of preeminence for aesthetic criteria of worth.

However, any such declaration of preeminence, even if it is resonant with classical human aspirations, represents a subordination of other legitimate claims. The ranking of claims of value is an unfortunate capitulation to the tyranny of theories of choice. The weighting of values rationalizes trade-offs but denies human capabilities for pursuing unresolved conflicts in desire. When my granddaughters were young, they had best friends, a not particularly noteworthy fact except that each of them had not one but numerous best friends—each best friend, I assume, a better friend than the others. I came to recognize that by refusing to calibrate the values of highly valued things in a way that assigned unique preeminence to any one of them, my granddaughters imported wisdom into grammar.

The creation and contemplation of imaginative understanding are distinctively and gloriously human, but they are not alone in this. Adaptive improvement through deliberate problem solving is also an exquisite feature of human distinctiveness. Intelligence involves the beauties of crafting understandings of experience, as reflected in the grace of storytelling and the elegance of model building. It also involves the efficiencies of adaptation, as reflected in the use of experience for careful analysis and pragmatic improvement. The lessons of experience are both monuments to the splendor of human imagination and instruments of effective problem solving. In tribute to the wisdom of granddaughters, each of these components of human intelligence can be seen as more important than the other.

REFERENCES

Abegglen, J. C. (1958). *The Japanese Factory.* Glencoe, IL: Free Press.

Abrahamson, E. (1991). Managerial fads and fashions: The diffusion and rejection of innovations. *Academy of Management Review,* 16:586–612.

Adner, R., and D. Levinthal (2004). What is *not* a real option: Considering boundaries for the application of real options to business strategy. *Academy of Management Review,* 29:74–85.

Akerlof, G. A., and R. E. Kranton (2005). Identity and the economics of organizations. *Journal of Economic Perspectives,* 19:9–32.

Alchian, A. A. (1950). Uncertainty, evolution, and economic theory. *Journal of Political Economy,* 58:211–221.

Aldrich, H. (1979). *Organizations and Environments.* Eglewood Cliffs, NJ: Prentice Hall.

Aldrich, H., and M. Ruef (2006). *Organizations Evolving.* Thousand Oaks, CA: Sage.

Amabile, T. (1983). *The Social Psychology of Creativity.* New York, NY: Springer-Verlag.

American Heritage Dictionary of the English Language (1981). Boston, MA: Houghton Mifflin.

Anand, P. (1993). *Foundations of Rational Choice under Risk.* Oxford, UK: Oxford University Press.

Andersen, H. C. (1837). Kejserens nye Klæder. Translated and published in English as "The Emperor's New Clothes" in D. F. Frank and J. Frank, eds. (2003). *The Stories of Hans Christian Andersen,* Boston, MA: Houghton Mifflin, pp. 105–110.

Anderson, B. (1991). *Imagined Communities.* 2nd ed. London, UK: Verso.

Argote, L. (1999). *Organizational Learning: Creating, Retaining, and Transferring Knowledge.* Dordrecht, Neth.: Kluwer Academic Publishers.

Argote, L., and D. Epple (1990). Learning curves in manufacturing. *Science,* 247:920–924.

Argote, L., and G. Todorova (2007). Organizational learning. *International Review of Industrial and Organizational Psychology,* 22:193–234.

Argyris, C., and D. Schön (1978). *Organizational Learning.* Reading, MA: Addison-Wesley.

Aronson, S. H. (1977). Bell's electrical toy: What's the use? The sociology of early telephone usage. In I. de Sola Pool, ed., *The Social Impact of the Telephone.* Cambridge, MA: MIT Press, 15–39.

Arrow, K. (1972). *The Limits of Organization.* New York, NY: Norton.

Ashforth, B. E., and F. Mael (1989). Social identity theory and the organization. *Academy of Management Review,* 14:20–39.

Arthur, W. B. (1989). Competing technologies, increasing returns, and lock-in by historical events. *Economic Journal,* 99:116–131.

Augier M., and J. G. March (2001). Conflict of interest in theories of organization: Herbert A. Simon and Oliver E. Williamson. *Journal of Management and Governance,* 5:223–230.

——, eds. (2002). *The Economics of Choice, Change and Organization: Essays in Honor of Richard M. Cyert.* Cheltenham, UK: Edward Elgar.

—— (2008). Realism and comprehension in economics: A footnote to an exchange between Oliver E. Williamson and Herbert A. Simon. *Journal of Economic Behavior and Organization,* 66:95–105.

Bandura, A. (1977). *Social Learning Theory.* Englewood Cliffs, NJ: Prentice-Hall.

Barley, S. (1986). Technology as an occasion for structuring: Evidence from observations of CAT scanners and the social order of radiology departments. *Administrative Science Quarterly,* 31:78–108.

Barnett, W. P., and M. T. Hansen (1996). The Red Queen in organizational evolution. *Strategic Management Journal,* 17:139–157.

Bartel, C. A., and R. Garud (2009). The role of narratives in sustaining organizational innovation. *Organization Science,* 20:107–117.

Barthes, R. (1977). *Image, Music, Text.* New York, NY: Hill and Wang.

Bartholomew, D. J. (1982). *Stochastic Models for Social Processes.* 3rd ed. Chichester, UK: Wiley.

Baum, J. A. C., and K. B. Dahlin (2007). Aspiration performance and railroads' patterns of learning from train wrecks and crashes. *Organization Science,* 18:368–385.

Baum, J. A. C., and J. V. Singh, eds. (1994). *The Evolutionary Dynamics of Organizations.* New York, NY: Oxford University Press.

Baumard, P., and W. H. Starbuck (2005). Learning from failures: Why it may not happen. *Long Range Planning,* 38:281–298.

Beauvoir, S. de ([1948] 1980). *The Ethics of Ambiguity.* Secaucus, NJ: Citadel.

Becker, H. (1963). *Outsiders: Studies in the Sociology of Deviance.* New York, NY: Free Press.

—— (1984). Moral entrepreneurs: The creation and enforcement of deviant categories. In D. Kelly, ed., *Deviant Behavior: A Text-Reader in the Sociology of Deviance.* New York, NY: St. Martin's, pp. 21–28.

Becker, M. C. (2004). Organizational routines: A review of the literature. *Industrial and Corporate Change,* 13:643–677.

Becker, M., T. Knudsen, and J. G. March (2006). Schumpeter, Winter, and the sources of novelty. *Industrial and Corporate Change,* 15:353–371.

Beecher-Monas, E. (2007). Marrying diversity and independence in the board room: Just how far have you come, baby? *Oregon Law Review,* 86:373–412.

Bennett, W. L., and M. S. Feldman (1981). *Reconstructing Reality in the Courtroom: Justice and Judgment in American Culture.* New Brunswick, NJ: Rutgers University Press.

Berger, P. L., and T. Luckmann. (1967). *The Social Construction of Reality: A Treatise in the Sociology of Knowledge.* Garden City, NY: Anchor.

Bergevärn, L-E., F. Mellomvik, and O. Olson (1998). Institutionalization of municipal accounting—A comparative study between Sweden and Norway." In N. Brunsson and J. P. Olsen, eds., *Organizing Organizations.* Bergen, Norway: Fagbokforlaget, pp. 279–302.

Bitney, D. (1969). Vico's new science of myth. In G. Tagliacozzo and H. V. White, eds., *Giambattista Vico: An International Symposium.* Baltimore, MD: Johns Hopkins University Press, pp. 259–277.

Blumer, H. (1969). *Symbolic Interactionism: Perspective and Method.* Englewood Cliffs, NJ: Prentice-Hall.

Bowman, E., and D. Hurry (1993). Strategy through the option lens: An integrated view of resource investments and the incremental-choice process. *Academy of Management Review,* 18:760–782.

Brandstätter, E., G. Gigerenzer, and R. Hertwig (2006). The priority heuristic: Making choices without trade-offs. *Psychological Review,* 113:409–432.

Brehmer, B. (1980). In one word: Not from experience. *Acta Psychologica,* 45:223–241.

Brown, S. L., and K. M. Eisenhardt. (1995). Product development: Past research, present findings, and future directions. *Academy of Management Review,* 20:343–378.

Bruner, J. (1996). *The Culture of Education.* Cambridge, MA: Harvard University Press.

Burt, R. S. (1987). Social contagion and innovation: Cohesion versus structural equivalence. *American Journal of Sociology,* 92:1287–1335.

Bush, R. R., and F. Mosteller (1955). *Stochastic Models for Learning.* New York, NY: Wiley.

Camerer, C. (2008). The case for mindful economics. In A. Caplin and A. Schotter, eds., *The Foundations of Positive and Normative Economics*. Oxford, UK: Oxford University Press, pp. 43–69.

Camerer, C. F., G. Loewenstein, and M. Rabin (2004). *Advances in Behavioral Economics*. New York, NY: Russell Sage.

Carroll, G. R., and M. T. Hannan (1989). Density dependence in the evolution of populations of newspaper organizations. *American Sociological Review*, 54:524–541.

—— (2000). *The Demography of Corporations and Industries*. Princeton, NJ: Princeton University Press.

Chekhov, A. (1979). *Anton Chekhov's Short Stories* (selected and edited by R. E. Matlaw). New York: Norton.

Chen, E. L., and R. Katila (2008). Rival intepretations of balancing exploration and exploitation: Simultaneous or sequential? In S. Shane, ed., *Handbook of Technology and Innovation Management*. New York, NY: Wiley, pp. 197–214.

Cicourel, A. V. (1974). *Cognitive Sociology: Language and Meaning in Social Interaction*. New York, NY: Free Press.

Cohen M. D., R. Burkhart, G. Dosi, M. Egidi, L. Marengo, M. Warglien, S. Winter (1996). Routines and other recurring action patterns of organizations: Contemporary research issues, *Industrial and Corporate Change*, 5:653–698.

Cohen, M. D., and L. S. Sproull, eds. (1996). *Organizational Learning*. Thousand Oaks, CA: Sage.

Cohen, W. M., and D. A. Levinthal (1989). Innovation and learning: The two faces of R&D. *Economic Journal*, 99:569–590.

—— (1990). Absorptive capacity: A new perspective on learning and innovation. *Administrative Science Quarterly*, 15:128–152.

Coleman, J. S. (1990). *Foundations of Social Theory*. Cambridge, MA: Belknap Press.

Collingwood, R. G. (1993). *The Idea of History*. Oxford, UK: Clarendon Press.

Conell, C., and S. Cohn (1995). Learning from other people's actions: Environmental variation and diffusion in French coal mining strikes, 1890–1935. *American Journal of Sociology*, 101:366–403.

Cyert, R. M., and J. G. March (1963). *A Behavioral Theory of the Firm*. Englewood Cliffs, NJ: Prentice-Hall.

Czarniawska, B. (1997). *Narrating the Organization: Dramas of Institutional Identity.* Chicago, IL: University of Chicago Press.
—— (2008). *A Theory of Organizing.* Cheltenham, UK: Edward Elgar.
Czarniawska, B., and B. Joerges (1996). Travels of ideas. In B. Czarniawska and G. Sevón, eds., *Translating Organizational Change.* Berlin: de Gruyter, pp. 13–48.
Czarniawska, B., and G. Sevón, eds. (1996). *Translating Organizational Change.* Berlin, Ger.: De Gruyter.
——, eds. (2005). *Global Ideas: How Ideas, Objects and Practices Travel in the Global Economy.* Malmö, Swed., and Copenhagen, Den.: Liber AB and Copenhagen Business School Press.
Darwin, C. ([1859] 2006). *The Origin of the Species, a Variorum Text,* edited by M. Peckham. Philadelphia, PA: University of Pennsylvania Press.
David, P. A. (1991). The hero and the herd in technological history: Reflections on Thomas Edison and "The Battle of the Systems." In P. Higgonet, D. S. Landes, and H. Rosovsky, eds., *Favorites of Fortune: Technology, Growth, and Economic Development since the Industrial Revolution.* Cambridge, MA: Harvard University Press, pp. 72–119.
Dawes, R. M., D. Faust, and P. E. Meehl (1989). Clinical versus actuarial judgment. *Science,* 243:1668–1674.
Denrell, J. (2007). Adaptive learning and risk taking, *Psychological Review,* 114:177–187.
—— (2008). Organizational risk taking: Adaptation versus variable risk preferences. *Industrial and Corporate Change,* 17:427–466.
Denrell, J., and C. Fang (2007). Success as a signal of poor judgment. Unpublished ms.
Denrell, J., and J. G. March (2001). Adaptation as information restriction: The hot stove effect. *Organization Science,* 12:523–538.
Deutsch, K. W. (1963). *The Nerves of Government.* Glencoe, IL: Free Press.
Dierkes, M., A. Berthoin Antal, J. Child, and I. Nonaka, eds. (2001). *Handbook of Organizational Learning and Knowledge.* Oxford, UK: Oxford University Press.

DiMaggio, P., and W. W. Powell (1983). The iron cage revisited: Institutional isomorphism and collective rationality in organizational fields. *American Sociological Review,* 48:147–160.

Djelic, M.-L. (1998). *Exporting the American Model: The Postwar Transformation of European Business.* Oxford, UK: Oxford University Press.

Dosi, G. (1988). Sources, procedures, and microeconomic effects of innovation. *Journal of Economic Literature,* 26:1120–1171.

Dosi, G., and L. Marengo (2007). On the evolutionary and behavioral theories of organizations: A tentative roadmap. *Organization Science,* 18:491–502.

Dosi, G., L. Marengo, A. Bassanini, and M. Valente (1999). Norms as emergent properties of adaptive learning: The case of economic routines, *Journal of Evolutionary Economics,* 9:5–26.

Durkheim, E. (1973). *On Morality and Society.* Trans. R. N. Bellah. Chicago, IL: University of Chicago Press.

Dworkin, R. (1986). *Law's Empire.* Cambridge, MA: Harvard University Press.

Eisenstadt, S. N. (2006). Multiple Modernen im Zeitalter der Globalisierung. In T. Schwinn, ed., *Die Vielfalt und Einheit der Modernen: kultur- und structurvergleichende analysen.* Wiesbaden, Ger.: VS Verlag für Sozialwissenschaften, pp. 37–62.

Etheredge, L. S. (1985). *Can Governments Learn? American Foreign Policy and Central American Revolutions.* New York, NY: Pergamon.

Fang, C., J. Lee, and M.. A. Schilling (forthcoming). Balancing exploration and exploitation through structural design: The isolation of subgroups and organization learning. *Organization Science.*

Fang, C., and D. Levinthal (2009). Near-term liability of exploitation: Exploration and exploitation in multistage problems. *Organization Science,* 20:538–551.

Feldman, M. S. (1989). *Order without Design: Information Production and Policy Making.* Stanford, CA: Stanford University Press.

—— (2000). Organizational routines as a source of continuous change. *Organization Science,* 11:611–629.

Feldman, M. S., and J. G. March (1981). Information in organizations as signal and symbol. *Administrative Science Quarterly,* 26:171–186.

Feldman, M. S., and B. T. Pentland (2003). Reconceptualizing organizational routines as a source of flexibility and change. *Administrative Science Quarterly,* 48:94–118.

Feller, W. (1968). *An Introduction to Probability Theory and Its Applications.* Vol. 1. 3rd ed. New York, NY: Wiley.

Fischhoff, B. (1975). Hindsight/foresight: The effect of outcome knowledge on judgment uncertainty. In T. S. Wallsten, ed., *Cognitive Processes in Choice and Decision Behavior.* Hillsdale, NJ: Erlbaum.

Foucault, M. (1961). *Folie et déraison: Histoire de la folie à l'âge classique.* Paris, Fr.: Librairie Plon.

—— (1975). *Surveiller et punir: Naissance de la prison.* Paris, Fr.: Gallimard.

Friedland, R., and R. R. Alford (1991). Bringing society back in: Symbols, practices and institutional contradictions. In W. W. Powell and P. J. DiMaggio, eds., *The New Institutionalism in Organizational Analysis.* Chicago, IL: University of Chicago Press, pp. 232–263.

Gabriel, Y., ed. (2004). *Myths, Stories, and Organizations: Premodern Narratives for Our Times.* Oxford, UK: Oxford University Press.

Gagliardi, P., and B. Czarniawska, eds. (2006). *Management Education and the Humanities.* Cheltenham, UK: Edward Elgar.

Galaskiewiecz, J., and R. S. Burt (1991). Interorganizational contagion in corporate philanthropy. *Administrative Science Quarterly,* 36:88–105.

Galunic, D. C., and S. Rodan (1998). Resource recombinations in the firm: Structures and the potential for Schumpeterian innovation. *Strategic Management Journal,* 18:1193–1201.

Garfinkel, H. (1967). *Studies in Ethnomethodology.* Englewood Cliffs, NJ: Prentice-Hall.

Garud, R., P. R. Nayyar, and Z. Shapira, eds. (1997). *Technological Innovation: Oversights and Foresights.* New York, NY: Cambridge University Press.

Gary, M. S., G. Dosi, and D. Lovallo (2008). Boom and bust behavior: On the persistence of strategic decision biases. In G. P. Hodgkinson and W. H. Starbuck, eds., *The Oxford Handbook of Organizational Decision Making*. Oxford, UK: Oxford University Press, pp. 33–55.

Gavetti, G., and D. Levinthal (2000). Looking forward and looking backward: Cognitive and experiential search. *Administrative Science Qaurterly,* 45:113–137.

Gavetti, G., D. Levinthal, and J. W. Rivkin (2005). Strategy-making in novel and complex worlds: The power of analogy. *Strategic Management Journal,* 26:691–712.

Gavetti, G., and M. Warglien (2007). Recognizing the new: A multi-agent model of analogy in strategic decision-making. Unpublished ms.

Geertz, C. (1973). Thick description: Toward an interpretive theory of culture. In C. Geertz, *The Interpretation of Cultures: Selected Essays*. New York, NY: Basic Books, pp. 3–30.

Geman, S., E. Bienenstock, and R. Doursat (1992). Neural networks and the bias/variance dilemma. *Neural Computation,* 4:1–58.

George, A. L., and T. McKeown (1985). Case studies and theories of organizational decision making. In R. F. Coulam and R. A. Smith, eds., *Advances in Information Processing in Organizations*. Vol. 2. Greenwich, CT: JAI Press, pp. 21–58.

Gherardi, S. (2006). *Organizational Knowledge: The Texture of Workplace Learning*. Oxford, UK: Blackwell.

Gibbons, R. (1992). *Game Theory for Applied Economists*. Princeton, NJ: Princeton University Press.

—— (2003). Team theory, garbage cans, and real organizations. *Industrial and Corporate Change,* 12:753–787.

Gibbons, R., and J. Roberts (2008). *Handbook of Organizational Economics*. Princeton, NJ: Princeton University Press.

Gigerenzer, G. (2000). *Adaptive Thinking: Rationality in the Real World*. Oxford, UK: Oxford University Press.

Gigerenzer, G., and H. Brighton (2009). Homo heuristicus: Why biased minds make better inferences. *Topics in Cognitive Science,* 1:107–143.

Gilboa, I., and D. Schmeidler (2001). *A Theory of Case-based Decisions*. Cambridge, UK: Cambridge University Press.

Gittins, J. C. (1989). *Multi-armed Bandit Allocation Indices*. New York, NY: Wiley.

Gladwell, M. (2000). *The Tipping Point*. Boston, MA: Little, Brown.

Golden-Biddle, K., and K. D. Locke (1997). *Composing Qualitative Research*. Thousand Oaks, CA: Sage.

Gould, S. J. (2002). *The Structure of Evolutionary Theory*. Cambridge, MA: Harvard University Press.

Gouldner, A W. (1954). *Patterns of Industrial Bureaucracy*. Glencoe, IL: Free Press.

Granovetter, M., and R. Soong (1983). Threshold models of diffusion and collective behavior. *Journal of Mathematical Sociology*, 9:165–179.

Gray, V. (1973). Innovation in the states: A diffusion study. *American Political Science Review*, 67:1174–1185.

Greene, W. H. (2008). *Econometric Analysis*. 6th ed. Upper Saddle River, NJ: Pearson/Prentice Hall.

Greenwood, R., and R. Suddaby (2006). Institutional entrepreneurship in a mature field: the Big 5 accounting firms. *Academy of Management Journal*, 49:27–48.

Greenwood, R., R. Suddaby, and C. R. Hinings (2002). The role of professional associations in the transformation of institutionalized fields. *Academy of Management Journal*, 45:58–80.

Greve, H. R. (2003). *Organizational Learning from Performance Feedback*. Cambridge. UK: Cambridge University Press.

Gul, F., and W. Pesendorfer (2008). The case for mindless economics. In A. Caplin and A. Schotter, eds., *The Foundations of Positive and Normative Economics*. Oxford, UK: Oxford University Press, pp. 3–42.

Günther, K. (1993). *The Sense of Appropriateness: Application Discourses in Morality and Law*. Albany, NY: State University of New York Press.

Halberstam, D. (1972). *The Best and the Brightest*. Random House: New York, NY.

Hannan, M. T. (1998). Rethinking age dependence in organizational mortality rate: Logical formalization. *American Journal of Sociology,* 104:85–123.

Hannan, M. T., and J. Freeman (1989). *Organizational Ecology.* Cambridge, MA: Harvard University Press.

Harrison, J. R., and J. G. March (1984). Decision making and post-decision surprises, *Administrative Science Quarterly,* 29:26–42.

Hastie, T., R. Tibshirani, and J. Friedman (2001). *The Elements of Statistical Learning: Data Mining, Inference, and Prediction.* New York, NY: Springer.

Hatchuel, A., and B. Weil (1995). *Experts in Organizations: A Knowledge-Based Perspective on Organizational Change.* Berlin, Ger.: Walter de Gruyter.

Haunschild, P. R., and A. S. Miner (1997). Modes of interorganizational imitation: The effects of outcome salience and uncertainty. *Administrative Science Quarterly,* 42:472–500.

Hebb, D. O. (1949). *The Organization of Behavior.* New York, NY: Wiley.

Hedrick, P. W. (1982). Genetic hitchhiking: A new factor in evolution? *BioScience,* 32:845–853.

Herbst, P.G. (1970). *Behavioural Worlds: The Study of Single Cases.* London, UK: Tavistock.

Hernes, T. (2008). *Understanding Organization as Process: Theory for a Tangled World.* London, UK: Routledge.

Hirschman, A. O. (1970). *Exit, Voice, and Loyalty.* Cambridge, MA: Harvard University Press.

Hodgkinson, G. P., and W. H. Starbuck, eds. (2008). *The Oxford Handbook of Organizational Decision Making.* Oxford, UK: Oxford University Press.

Hoffman, A. (1999). Institutional evolution and change: Environmentalism and the U. S. chemical industry. *Academy of Management Journal,* 42:351–371.

Hogarth, R. M., and N. Karelaia (2005). Ignoring information in binary choice with continuous variables: When is less "more"? *Journal of Mathematical Psychology,* 49:115–124.

Holahan, J., Weil, A., Wiener, J. M., eds. (2003). *Federalism and Health Policy.* Washington, DC: Urban Institute Press.

Holden, R. T. (1986). The contagiousness of aircraft hijacking. *American Journal of Sociology,* 91:874–904.

Holland, J. H. (1975). *Adaptation in Natural and Artificial Systems.* Ann Arbor, MI: University of Michigan Press.

Holmqvist, M. (2008). *The Institutionalization of Social Welfare: A Study of Medicalizing Management.* New York, NY: Routledge.

Hoopes, D. G., and T. L. Madsen (2008). A capability-based view of competitive heterogeneity. *Industrial and Corporate Change,* 17:393–426.

Huber, G. P. (1991). Organizational learning: The contributing processes and the literatures. *Organization Science,* 2:88–115.

Hutchinson, J. M. C., and G. Gigerenzer (2005). Simple heuristics and rules of thumb: Where psychologists and behavioural biologists might meet. *Behavioural Processes,* 69:97–124.

Jeppesen, L. B., and K. R. Lakhani (2009). Attracting needles from the haystack: The importance of marginality in a broadcast search problem solving process. Unpublished ms.

Kahneman, D., and D. Lovallo (1993). Timid choices and bold forecasts: A cognitive perspective on risk taking. *Management Science,* 39:17–31.

Kahneman, D., and A. Tversky (1979). Prospect theory: An analysis of decision under risk. *Econometrica,* 47:263–291.

Kauffman, S. A., and S. Johnsen (1992). Co-evolution to the edge of chaos: Coupled fitness landscapes, poised states, and co-evolutionary avalanches. In C. G. Langton, L. Taylor, J. D. Farmer, and S. Rasmussen, eds., *Artificial Life II,* Redwood City, CA: Addison Wesley, pp. 325–368.

Kaufman, H. (1960). *The Forest Ranger.* Baltimore, MD: Johns Hopkins University Press.

Kayes, D. C. (2002). Experiential learning and its critics: Preserving the role of experience in management learning and education. *Academy of Management Learning and Education,* 1:137–149.

Kieser, A. (1997). Rhetoric and myth in management fashion. *Organizations,* 4:49–74.

—— (2002). Managers as marionettes? Using fashion theories to explain the success of consultants. In M. Kipping and L. Engwall, eds., *Management Consulting: Emergence and Dynamics of a Knowledge Industry,* Oxford, UK: Oxford University Press, pp. 167–183.

Kolb, D. A. (1984). *Experiential Learning: Experience as a Source of Learning Development.* Englewood Cliffs, NJ: Prentice Hall.

Kosnik, L.-R. D. (2008). Refusing to budge: A confirmatory bias in decision making. *Mind and Society,* 7:193–214.

Krachardt, D., and M. Killduff, M. (1990). Friendship patterns and culture: The control of organizational diversity. *American Anthropologist,* 91:142–154.

Kreps, D. M. (1990a). Corporate culture and economic theory. In J. E. Alt and K. A. Shepsle, eds., *Perspectives on Political Economy.* Cambridge, UK: Cambridge University Press, pp. 90–143.

—— (1990b). *Game Theory and Economic Modeling.* Oxford, UK: Clarendon Press.

Krieger, S. (1979). *Hip Capitalism.* Beverly Hills, CA: Sage.

Kuhn, T. S. (1962). *The Structure of Scientific Revolutions.* Chicago, IL: University of Chicago Press.

—— (1977). *The Essential Tension: Selected Studies in Scientific Tradition and Change.* Chicago, IL: University of Chicago Press.

Lamberg, J.-A., A. Laukia, and J. Ojala (2008). The origins of success: A qualitative meta-analysis of the evolution of Nokia. Paper presented at the Academy of Management meetings in Anaheim, CA.

Lave, C. A., and J. G. March (1975). *An Introduction to Models in the Social Sciences.* New York, NY: Harper and Row.

Lenz, R. (1981). Determinants of organizational performance: An interdisciplinary review. *Strategic Management Review,* 2:131–154.

Levinthal, D. A. (1991). Random walks and organizational mortality. *Administrative Science Quarterly,* 36:397–420.

Levinthal, D. A., and J. G. March (1993). The myopia of learning. *Strategic Management Journal,* 14:95–112.

Levinthal, D.A., and J. Myatt (1994). Co-evolution of capabilities and industry: The evolution of mutual fund processing. *Strategic Management Journal,* 15:45–62.

Levinthal, D. A., and H. E. Posen (2007). Myopia of selection: Does organizational adaptation limit the efficacy of population selection?" *Administrative Science Quarterly*, 52:586–620.

Lévi-Strauss, C. (1966). *The Savage Mind*. London, UK: Weidenfeld and Nicolson.

—— (1979). *Myth and Meaning*. New York, NY: Schocken Books.

Levitt B., and March, J. G. (1988). Organizational learning. *Annual Review of Sociology*, 14:319–340.

Levy, S. (2003). Out of left field. *Newsweek*, April 21.

Loasby, B. (1999). *Knowledge, Institutions and Evolution in Economics*. London, UK: Routledge.

Lord, C. G., L. Ross, and M. R. Lepper (1979). Biased assimilation and attitude polarization: The effect of prior theories on subsequently considered evidence. *Journal of Personality and Social Psychology*, 37:2098–2109.

Lovie, S. (2005). History of mathematical learning theory. In *Encyclopedia of Statistics in Behavioral Science*. Vol. 2. New York, NY: Wiley, pp. 861–864.

Luce, R.D., and H. Raiffa (1957). *Games and Decisions*. New York, NY: Wiley.

Machina, M. J. (1987). Choice under uncertainty: Problems solved and unsolved. *Journal of Economic Perspectives*, 1:121–154.

Mahajan, V., and Y. Wind (1986). *Innovation Diffusion Models of New Product Acceptance*. Cambridge, MA: Ballinger.

Malthus, T. R. ([1798] 2001). *An Essay on the Principle of Population*. London, UK: Electric Book Co.

Mansfield, E. (1961). Technical change and the rate of imitation. *Econometrica*, 29:741–766.

March, J. G. (1988). *Decisions and Organizations*, Oxford, UK: Blackwell.

—— (1992). The war is over and the victors have lost. *Journal of Socio-Economics*, 21:261–267.

—— (1994). *A Primer on Decision Making: How Decisions Happen*. New York, NY: Free Press.

—— (1999a). A learning perspective on some dynamics of institutional integration. In M. Egeberg and P. Lægreid, eds., *Organiz-*

ing Political Institutions: Essays for Johan P. Olsen. Oslo, Nor.: Scandinavian University Press, pp. 129–155.

—— (1999b). Les mythes du management, *Gérer et Comprendre,* no. 57 (September): 4–12.

—— (1999c). *The Pursuit of Organizational Intelligence*. Oxford, UK: Blackwell.

—— (2004). Experiential knowledge and academic knowledge in management education. In G. Garel and E. Godelier, eds., *Enseigner le management*. Paris, Fr.: Lavosier, pp. 13–17.

—— (2008). *Explorations in Organizations*. Stanford, CA: Stanford University Press.

March, J. G., and J. C. March (1977). Almost random careers: The Wisconsin school superintendency, 1940–1972. *Administrative Science Quarterly,* 22:377–409.

March, J. G., and J. P. Olsen (1975). The uncertainty of the past: Organizational learning under ambiguity. *European Journal of Political Research,* 3:147–171.

—— (1976). *Ambiguity and Choice in Organizations*. Bergen, Nor.: Universitetsforlaget.

—— (1989). *Rediscovering Institutions: The Organizational Basis of Politics*. New York, NY: Free Press.

—— (1995). *Democratic Governance*. New York, NY: Free Press.

—— (2006a). Elaborating the new institutionalism. In R. A. W. Rhodes, S. Binder, and B. Rockman, eds., *The Oxford Handbook of Political Institutions*. Oxford, UK: Oxford University Press, pp. 3–20.

—— (2006b). The logic of appropriateness. In M. Moran, M. Rein, and R. E. Goodin, eds., *The Oxford Handbook of Public Policy.* Oxford: Oxford University Press, pp. 689–708.

March, J. G., M. Schulz, and X. Zhou (2000). *The Dynamics of Rules: Change in Written Organizational Codes*. Stanford, CA: Stanford University Press.

March, J. G., and G Sevón (1984). Gossip, information, and decision-making. In L. S. Sproull and J. P. Crecine, eds., *Advances in Information Processing in Organizations*. Vol. 1. Greenwich, CT: JAI Press, pp. 95–107.

March, J. G., and Z. Shapira (1987). Managerial perspectives on risk and risk taking. *Management Science,* 33:1404–1418.

—— (1992). Variable risk preferences and the focus of attention. *Psychological Review,* 99:172–183.

March, J. G., and H. A. Simon (1958). *Organizations.* New York, NY: Wiley.

March, J. G., L. S. Sproull, and M. Tamuz (1991). Learning from samples of one or fewer. *Organization Science,* 2:1–13.

March, J. G., and R. I. Sutton (1997). Organizational performance as a dependent variable. *Organization Science,* 8:697–706.

March, K. S. (2002). *"If Each Comes Halfway".* Ithaca, NY: Cornell University Press.

Mayr, E. (1963). *Population, Species, and Evolution.* Cambridge, MA: Harvard University Press.

—— (1982). *The Growth of Biological Thought. Diversity, Evolution, and Inheritance.* Cambridge, MA: Belknap Press.

McGrath, R. (1999). Falling forward: Real options reasoning and entrepreneurial failure. *Academy of Management Review,* 22:974–996.

Merton, Robert K. (1968). The Matthew effect in science. *Science,* 159:56–63.

Mezias, J. M., and W. H. Starbuck (2003). Studying the accuracy of managers' perceptions: A research odyssey. *British Journal of Management* 14:2–17.

Milan, L., and M. P. Kriger (1998). Making sense of managerial wisdom. *Journal of Management Inquiry,* 7:242–251.

Milgrom, P., and J. Roberts (1992). *Economics, Organization and Management.* Englewood Cliffs, NJ: Prentice-Hall.

Mill, J. S. ([1861] 1962). *Considerations on Representative Government.* South Bend, IN: Gateway Editions.

Miller, D. (1994). What happens after success: The perils of excellence. *Journal of Management Studies,* 31:325–358.

Miller, N. E., and J. Dollard (1941). *Social Learning and Imitation.* New Haven, CT: Yale University Press.

Miner, A. S., P. R. Haunschild, and A. Schwab (2003). Experience and convergence: Curiosities and speculation. *Industrial and Corporate Change,* 12:789–813.

Minsky, M. (1963). Steps toward artificial intelligence. In E. A. Feigenbaum and J. Feldman, eds., *Computers and Thought*. New York, NY: McGraw-Hill, pp. 406–450.

Mirowski, P. (1989). *More Heat Than Light: Economics as Social Physics, Physics as Nature's Economics*. Cambridge, UK: Cambridge University Press.

Mohr, L. B. (1985). The reliability of the case study as a source of information. In R. F. Coulam and R. A. Smith, eds., *Advances in Information Processing in Organizations*. Vol 2. Greenwich, CT: JAI Press, pp. 65–94.

Mowrer, R. R., and S. B. Klein, eds. (2001). *Handbook of Contemporary Learning Theories*. Mahwah, NJ: Erlbaum.

Nehaniv, C. L., and K. Dautenhahn, eds. (2007). *Imitation and Social Learning in Robots, Humans, and Animals: Behavioural, Social, and Communicative Dimensions*. Cambridge, UK: Cambridge University Press.

Nelson, R., and S. G. Winter (1982). *An Evolutionary Theory of Economic Change*. Cambridge, MA.: Harvard University Press.

—— (2002). Evolutionary theorizing in economics. *Journal of Economic Literature, 16(2)*: 23–46.

Newell, S., J. Swan, and K. Kautz (2001). The role of funding bodies in the creation and diffusion of management fads and fashions. *Organization*, 8:97–120.

Nickerson, R. S. (1998). Confirmation bias: A ubiquitous phenomenon in many guises. *Review of General Psychology*, 2:175–220.

Nietzsche, F. W. (1957). *The Use and Abuse of History*. Trans. A. Collins. Indianapolis, IN: Bobbs-Merrill.

—— (1997). *Human, All Too Human*. Stanford, CA: Stanford University Press.

Nohria, N., and R. Gulati (1996). Is slack good or bad for innovation? *Academy of Management Journal*, 39:1245–1264

Nonaka, I., and H. Takeuchi (1995). *The Knowledge-Creating Company*. New York, NY: Oxford University Press.

Nooteboom, B. (2000). *Learning and Innovation in Organizations and Economies*. Oxford, UK: Oxford University Press.

Nooteboom, B., and E. Stam, eds. (2008). *Micro-foundations for Innovation Policy*. Chicago, IL: University of Chicago Press.

North, D. C. (1990). *Institutions, Institutional Change and Economic Performance*. Cambridge, MA: Harvard University Press.

Oberoi, H. (1994). *The Construction of Religious Boundaries: Culture, Identity, and Diversity in the Sikh Tradition*. Chicago, IL: University of Chicago Press.

Obstfeld, D. (2005). Social networks, the tertius iungens orientation, and involvement in innovation. *Administrative Science Quarterly*, 50:100–130.

O'Connor, E. S. (2008). Exploration in organizations through literature: An introductory essay. In J. G. March, *Explorations in Organizations*. Stanford, CA: Stanford University Press, pp. 413–433.

Olsen, J. P. (2009). Change and continuity: An institutional approach to institutions of democratic government. *European Political Science Review*, 1:3–32.

Olsen, J. P., and B. G. Peters (1996). *Lessons from Experience: Experiential Learning in Administrative Reforms in Eight Democracies*. Oslo, Nor.: Scandinavian University Press.

Padgett, J. F., and C. K. Ansell (1993). Robust action and the rise of the Medici, 1400–1434. *American Journal of Sociology*, 98:1250–1310.

Padgett, J. F., D. Lee, and N. Collier (2003). Economic production as chemistry. *Industrial and Corporate Change*, 12:843–878.

Padgett, J. F., and P. D. McLean (2006). Organizational invention and elite transformation: The birth of partnership systems in renaissance Florence. *American Journal of Sociology*, 111:1463–1568.

Page, S. E. (2007). *The Difference: How the Power of Diversity Creates Better Groups, Firms, Schools, and Societies*. Princeton, NJ: Princeton University Press.

Payne, J. W., J. R. Bettman, and E. J. Johnson (1993). *The Adaptive Decision Maker*. New York, NY: Cambridge University Press.

Payne, J. W., D. J. Laughhann, and R. L. Crum (1980). Translation of gambles and aspiration level effects in risky choice behavior. *Management Science*, 26:1039–1060.

—— (1981), Further tests of aspiration level effects in risky choice behavior. *Management Science*, 27:953–958.

Pentland, B. T. (1995). Grammatical models of organizational processes. *Organization Science,* 6:541–556.

Pentland, B. T., and H. H. Rueter (1994). Organizational routines as grammars of action. *Administrative Science Quarterly,* 39:484–510.

Perrow, C. (1984). *Normal Accidents.* New York, NY: Basic Books.

Pfeffer, J., and R. I. Sutton (2006). *Hard Facts, Dangerous Half-Truths, and Total Nonsense: Profiting from Evidence-Based Management.* Boston, MA: Harvard Business School Press.

Pisano, G. P., M. J. Bohmer, and A. C. Edmondson (2001). Organizational differences in rates of learning: Evidence from the adoption of minimally invasive cardiac surgery. *Management Science,* 47:752–768.

Podolny, J. M., T. E. Stuart, and M. T. Hannan (1996). Networks, knowledge, and niches: Competition in the worldwide semiconductor industry, 1984–1991. *American Journal of Sociology,* 102:659–689.

Polanyi, M. (1963). The potential theory of adsorption: Authority in science has its uses and its dangers. *Science,* 141:1010–1013.

Polkinghorne, D. (1988). *Narrative Knowing and the Human Sciences.* Albany, NY: State University of New York Press.

Potvin, C., M. Kraenzel, and G. Seutin, eds. (2001). *Protecting Biological Diversity: Roles and Responsibilities.* McGill-Queens University Press.

Powell, W. W., K. W. Koput, and L. Smith-Doerr (1996). Interorganizational collaboration and the locus of innovation: Networks of learning in biotechnology. *Administrative Science Quarterly,* 41:116–146.

Purdy, J., and B. Gray (2009). Conflicting logics, mechanisms of diffusion, and multilevel dynamics in emerging institutional fields. *Academy of Management Journal,* 52:355–380.

Raiffa, H. (1968). *Decision Analysis.* Reading, MA: Addison-Wesley.

Rao, H., C. Morrill, and M. N. Zald (2000). Power plays: How social movements and collective action create new organizational forms. In R. I. Sutton and B. M. Staw, eds., *Research in Organizational Behavior.* Vol. 22. Greenwich, CT: JAI Press, pp. 239–282.

Reagans, R., L. Argote, and D. Brooks (2005). Individual experience and experience working together. *Management Science,* 51:869–881.

Reich, R. B. (1985). The executive's new clothes. *New Republic,* May 13, 1985, pp. 23–28.

Reinganum, J. F. (1989). The timing of innovation: Research, development, and diffusion. In R. Schmalensee and R. D. Willig, eds., *Handbook of Industrial Organization.* New York, NY: North-Holland, pp. 849–908.

Ricoeur, P. (1965). *History and Truth.* Evanston, IL: Northwestern University Press.

Riveline, C. (2008). Zones aveugles. *Le Journal de l'École de Paris du Management,* 74:7.

Rodan, S. (2008). Organizational learning: Effects of (network) structure and (individual) strategy. *Computational and Mathematical Organization Theory,* 14:222–247.

Rodan, S., and C. Galunic (2004). More than network structure: How knowledge heterogeneity influences managerial performance and innovativeness. *Strategic Management Journal,* 25:541–556.

Roethlisberger, F. J., and W. J. Dickson (1939). *Management and the Worker.* Cambridge, MA: Harvard University Press.

Romano, R. (2002). *The Advantages of Competitive Federalism for Securities Regulation.* Washington, DC: American Enterprise Institute Press.

Romer, P. (1994). Economic growth and investment in children. *Daedalus,* 123:141–154.

Said, E. W. (1978). *Orientalism.* New York, NY: Vintage.

Sarbin, T. R. (1986). *Narrative Psychology: The Storied Nature of Human Conduct.* New York, NY: Praeger.

Sauer, B. A. (2003). *The Rhetoric of Risk: Technical Documentation in Hazardous Environments.* Mahwah, NJ: Erlbaum.

Schelling, T. C. (1971). Dynamic models of segregation. *Journal of Mathematical Sociology,* 1:143–186.

—— (1978). *Micromotives and Macrobehavior.* New York, NY: Norton.

Schumpeter, J. A. (1934). *The Theory of Economic Development.*

An Inquiry into Profits, Capital, Credit, Interest, and the Business Cycle. Cambridge, MA: Harvard University Press.

Schütz, A. (1967). *The Phenomenology of the Social World.* Evanston, IL: Northwestern University Press.

Scott, W. R. (1981). *Organizations: Rational, Natural and Open Systems.* Englewood Cliffs, NJ: Prentice Hall.

—— (2003). Institutional carriers: Reviewing modes of transporting ideas over time and space and considering their consequences. *Industrial and Corporate Change,* 12:879–894.

Scott, W. R., and J. W. Meyer, eds., 1983. *Institutional Environments and Organizations: Structural Complexity and Individualism.* Thousand Oaks, CA: Sage.

Selten, R. (1991). Evolution, learning and economic behavior. *Games and Economic Behavior,* 3:3–24.

Selznick, P. (1949). *TVA and the Grass Roots.* Berkeley, CA: University of California Press.

Senge, P. (1990). *The Fifth Discipline: The Art and Practice of the Learning Organization.* New York, NY: Random House.

Shklar, J. N. (1990). *The Faces of Injustice.* New Haven, CT: Yale University Press.

Simonton, D. K. (1995). Creativity as heroic: Risk, failure, and acclaim. In C. M. Ford and D. A. Gioia, eds., *Creative Action in Organizations.* Newbury Park, CA: Sage, pp. 88–93.

—— (1999). *Origins of Genius: Darwinian Perspectives on Creativity.* New York, NY: Oxford University Press.

Singh, J. V., D. J. Tucker, and R. J. House (1986). Organizational legitimacy and the liability of newness. *Administrative Science Quarterly,* 31:171–193.

Sitkin, S. B. (1992). Learning through failure: The strategy of small losses. *Research in Organizational Behavior,* 14:231–266.

Snow, C. P. (1959). *The Two Cultures and the Scientific Revolution.* New York, NY: Cambridge University Press.

Spergel, I. (1964). *Racketville, Slumtown, Haulberg: An Exploratory Study of Delinquent Subcultures.* Chicago, IL: University of Chicago Press.

Starbuck, W. H., M. L. Barnett, and P. Baumard (2008). Payoffs and pitfalls of strategic learning. *Journal of Economic Behavior and Organizations*, 66:7–21.

Starbuck, W. H., A. Greve, and B. L. T. Hedberg (1978). Responding to crises. *Journal of Business Administration*, 9:111–137.

Starbuck, W. H., and B. L. T. Hedberg (2001). How organizations learn from success and failure. In M. Dierkes, A. Berthoin Antal, J. Child, and I. Nonaka, eds., *Handbook of Organizational Learning and Knowledge*. Oxford, UK: Oxford University Press, pp. 327–350.

Staw, B.M. (1975). Attribution of the "causes" of performance: An alternative interpretation of cross-sectional research on organizations. *Organizational Behavior and Human Performance*, 13:414–432.

Sternberg, R. J., and R. K. Wagner, eds. (1986). *Practical Intelligence: Nature and Origins of Competence in the Everyday World*. New York, NY: Cambridge University Press.

Strang, D., and M. W. Macy (2001). In search of excellence: Fads, success stories, and adaptive emulation. *American Journal of Sociology*, 107:147–182.

Strang, D, and S. A. Soule (1998). Diffusion in organizations and social movements: From hybrid corn to poison pills. *Annual Review of Sociology*, 24:265–290.

Sturluson, Snorri (1984). *From the Sagas of the Norse Kings*. Oslo, Nor.: Dreyers Forlag.

Sutton, R. I. (2002). *Weird Ideas That Work*. New York, NY: Free Press.

Svejenova, S., C. Mazza, and M. Planellas (2007). Cooking up change in haute cuisine: Ferran Adrià as an institutional entrepreneur. *Journal of Organizational Behavior*, 28:539–561.

Tamuz, M. (1988). Monitoring dangers in the air: Studies in ambiguity and Information. Ph.D. diss., Stanford University.

Taubman, P. (2007). Failure to launch: In death of spy satellite program, lofty plans and unrealistic bids. *New York Times*, November 11, 2007.

Tetlock, P. E. (1992). The impact of accountability on judgment and choice: Toward a social contingency model. *Advances in Experimental Social Psychology*, 25:331–376.

—— (1999). Theory-driven reasoning about possible pasts and

probable futures: Are we prisoners of our preconceptions? *American Journal of Political Science,* 43:335–366.

Thaler, R. H. (1988). Anomalies: The winner's curse. *Journal of Economic Perspectives,* 2:191–202.

Uzzi, B. (1996). The sources and consequences of embeddedness for the economic performance of organizations: The network effect. *American Sociological Review,* 61:674–98.

Van de Ven, A. H. (1999). *The Innovation Journey.* New York, NY: Oxford University Press.

Van Maanen, J. (1988). *Tales of the Field.* Chicago, IL: University of Chicago Press.

—— (1995). *Representation in Ethnography.* Thousand Oaks, CA: Sage.

Vico, G. ([1725] 1961). *The New Science of Giambattista Vico.* Garden City, NY: Doubleday.

Volden, C., M. M. Ting, and D. P. Carpenter (2008). A formal model of learning and policy diffusion. *American Political Science Review,* 102:319–332.

von Neumann, J., and O. Morgenstern (1944). *The Theory of Games and Economic Behavior.* Princeton, NJ: Princeton University Press.

Vygotsky, L. S. ([1962] 1986). *Thought and Language.* Cambridge, MA: MIT Press.

Walker, C. R., and R. H. Guest (1952). *The Man on the Assembly Line.* Cambridge, MA: Harvard University Press.

Weick, K. E. (1995). *Sensemaking in Organizations.* Thousand Oaks, CA: Sage.

—— (1996). Drop your tools: An allegory for organizational studies. *Administrative Science Quarterly,* 41:301–313.

Weitzman, M. L. (1998). Recombinant growth. *Quarterly Journal of Economics,* 113:331–360.

Wells, D., A. J. Donnell, A. Thomas, M. S. Mills, M. Miller (2006). Creative deviance: A study of the relationship between creative behaviour and the social construct of deviance. *College Student Journal,* 40:74–77.

Westerlund, G., and S.-E. Sjøstrand (1979). *Organizational Myths.* New York, NY: Harper and Row.

White, H. (1987). *Tropics of Discourse: Essays in Cultural Criticism.* Baltimore, MD: Johns Hopkins University Press.

White, H. C. (1970). *Chains of Opportunity.* Cambridge, MA: Harvard University Press.

Whyte, W. F. (1943). *Street Corner Society.* Chicago, IL: University of Chicago Press.

Williamson, Oliver E. (1975). *Markets and Hierarchy: Analysis and Antitrust Implications.* New York, NY: Free Press.

Wilson, R. (1977). A bidding model of perfect competition. *Review of Economic Studies,* 44:511–518.

Winter, S. G. (1964). Economic "natural selection" and the theory of the firm. *Yale Economic Essays,* 4:225–272.

—— (1971). Satisficing, selection and the innovating remnant. *Quarterly Journal of Economics,* 85:237–61.

—— (1987). Knowledge and competence as strategic assets. In D. J. Teece, ed., *The Competitive Challenge: Strategies for Industrial Innovation and Renewal.* New York, NY: Harper and Row, pp. 159–184.

—— (2009). The replication perspective on productive knowledge. Unpublished ms.

Winter, S. G., G. Cattani, and A. Dorsch (2007). The value of moderate obsession: Insights from a new model of organizational search. *Organization Science,* 18:403–419.

Witt, U. (2003). *The Evolving Economy: Essays on the Evolutionary Approach to Economics.* Cheltenham, UK: Edward Elgar.

Zaleznick, A. (1989). The mythological structure and its impact. *Human Resource Management,* 28:267–278.

Zbaracki, M. J. (1998). The rhetoric and reality of total quality management. *Administrative Science Quarterly,* 43:602–636.

Zollo, M., and S. G. Winter (2002). Deliberate learning and the evolution of dynamic capabilities. *Organization Science,* 13:339–351.

Zucker, L. G. (1987). Institutional theories of organizations. *Annual Review of Sociology,* 13:443–464.

INDEX